You know your past, but God wants you to know a great future. Change is possible, and your future can be full of the life you always have desired. But first you need to learn how to "move on," and this is exactly what Dr. Cooper has accomplished through this book *Unfinished Business*. I ask you to do yourself and your future a favor and get this book today!

—JENTEZEN FRANKLIN
SENIOR PASTOR OF FREE CHAPEL IN
GAINESVILLE, GEORGIA,
AND *NEW YORK TIMES* BEST-SELLING
AUTHOR OF *FASTING*

Dr. David Cooper's book *Unfinished Business* provides Christians and non-Christians alike with a practical manual to confront life's constant changes, disappointments, and frustrations. While we can't always "get over it," Dr. Cooper shows us Christ's path to "get on with it." Richly sourced and deeply rooted in biblical principles, *Unfinished Business* guides readers with the same easy-to-understand yet insightful teachings I've heard Dr. Cooper deliver from his pulpit on Sunday mornings.

—NATHAN DEAL
GOVERNOR OF GEORGIA

A key to successful living is learning from the past but leaving the past in the past. Jesus taught us to "shake off the dust," and Dr. David Cooper gives us great insight and specific instruction in his wonderful book, teaching us how to be released from areas that hold us captive.

D0370307

This book will motivate you and set you free. An absolute must-read.

—DAVE RAMSEY
#1 *NEW YORK TIMES* BEST-SELLING AUTHOR

None of us are exempt from the difficulties and painful experiences of life. But in order to move forward and embrace new opportunities, we have to push past the pain and "keep it moving." *Unfinished Business* is a dynamic and compelling book that reveals how to do just that. Dr. David C. Cooper candidly explains how to recognize when you're carrying "dust" or residue that may be hindering your progress in life. Then he masterfully exposes how to "shake it off" and refuse to be a victim of anything, including repressed memories, your past, regrets, fear, disappointment, rejection, anger, resentment, and failure.

Unfinished Business is a must-read for those who are stagnant in life and don't know how to confront the negative, excess baggage that has them weighted down. This thought-provoking masterpiece by Dr. Cooper demonstrates how to "shake off the dust" of the past, move forward toward your divine destiny, and embrace all the wonderful blessings God has in store for your future!

—CREFLO DOLLAR
SENIOR PASTOR OF WORLD CHANGERS CHURCH
INTERNATIONAL
ATLANTA, GEORGIA

It has been said, "A fool will lose tomorrow reaching back for yesterday." But for many people the unresolved pain from yesterday seeks to rob them of hope for tomorrow. Imbued with an insatiable quest for life, Dr. David Cooper brings his skills to bear as a pastor, counselor, and author to say, "Enough!" You don't want to sit through a meal with mustard on your chin, nor do you want to go through life carrying dust from the past that keeps you from living a full life today. As Dr. Cooper says, "Shake off the dust and move on!"

Intensely succinct and wondrously perceptive, this book offers wisdom and practical instruction to all who seek to lay hold of the abundant life Christ has promised.

—Dr. Mark L. Williams
General overseer of the Church of God
(Cleveland, Tennessee)

David Cooper has written a book that will be so helpful to so many on so many levels that I cannot urge you strongly enough to get this book!

—Mark Rutland
Former president of Oral Roberts University
and author of *ReLaunch*

A wise person once said, and it is oft repeated, "The way you leave one situation is the way you enter the next one." We are quite skilled at swallowing our pains, disappointments, negative emotions, and living a less than fully conscious, fully awake life. The current culture has many distractions through which to numb the pain of unfinished business from the past, preventing us from getting past our past and living in the present. If the past is present, the present is locked in the past, and the pain causes us to devalue the possibility of anything changing in the future. What we bury alive stays alive.

What we refuse to face, we cannot erase. Whatever is held in the unconscious is in control, whether we like it or not.

Allowing God to search our hearts and reveal the hidden hurtful self-sabotaging pains from our yesterdays is an essential part of the process of letting go and moving on into our todays and tomorrows. Dr. David Cooper, in my estimation, is one of the finest voices in the kingdom of God today for the cure of the soul and for healing unfinished business. His ability to integrate solid theology with sound psychological principles for real transformative change is evident in the many people he has come alongside by the Spirit to enable them to experience God's healing grace and empowerment. His expertise in the people-helping business will become immediately evident as you read each line of this monumental work.

Unfinished Business is a lifelong learning manual for every child of God who is weary of reliving the past, regretting the present, and recoiling from a devalued future as a result. It will take you on a journey to wholeness and well-being by showing how Jesus's strategic insight into the solutions for your dilemma will help get you past your past, whatever that encompasses and whatever it contains. *Unfinished Business* will provide fresh insight again and again as you learn to face the self-sabotaging strategies that hinder you from allowing God to set your feet in a large place. If you're ready to live the life God intends for you, this book will help you take the necessary steps to arrive there!

—MARK J. CHIRONNA, MA, PHD,
FOUNDER AND SENIOR PASTOR OF CHURCH ON THE
LIVING EDGE
ORLANDO, FLORIDA

I don't particularly like the term "ordinary people," but most of us are. Dr. David Cooper has been my friend for more than twenty years, and I've often wondered how I got to know such a talented and charming individual. The good thing is, he's "extraordinary" enough to be recognized by his peers and praised for his talents and "ordinary" enough to be able to relate to everyone. Everyone experiences change. Dr. Cooper's new book, *Unfinished Business*, will not only help you get through change but also will absolutely help you to excel in it!

—DOYLE DYKES
RENOWNED GUITARIST AND RECORDING ARTIST

Dr. Cooper is a multidimensional kingdom man. A well-known pastor, noted teacher, and dynamic preacher, he is also a talented musician. He has been my pastor for twenty years, but more than that, David Cooper has been a trusted friend. Teaching from the pulpit of Mount Paran Church in Atlanta, Georgia, Dr. Cooper has imparted truth, faith, and hope to the thousands of people each Sunday who come to worship.

A great encourager, Dr. Cooper believes that the fulfilled life is the surrendered life. The need to conquer fear, depression, regrets, confusion, and disappointments are vital to the successful Spirit-filled life. He teaches that taking every thought captive opens the possibilities for healing and true freedom. Over the years I have gleaned wisdom and encouragement from Dr. Cooper's deep knowledge of Scripture and its application to contemporary living.

Unfinished Business will empower the reader with ways to overcome wrong thinking, a life of regrets, and prolonged worry. I can promise that these chapters will be spirit-lifters and an aid to healthy recovery. The principles taught within these pages will empower the reader to examine their problems and take action in order to go to their next season, assignment, or opportunity. Through this journey to "shake off the dust" in your life, Dr. David Cooper will become your mentor, encourager, and new friend. By all means, read this book.

—ANN PLATZ
AUTHOR, SPEAKER, AND NOTED INTERIOR DESIGNER

CHANGE
YOUR THINKING,
DEAL WITH
YOUR PAST, AND
MOVE ON

unfinished
business

CHANGE
YOUR THINKING,
DEAL WITH
YOUR PAST, AND
MOVE ON

unfinished
business

DAVID C. COOPER,DMin

CHARISMA HOUSE

Most CHARISMA HOUSE BOOK GROUP products are available at special quantity discounts for bulk purchase for sales promotions, premiums, fund-raising, and educational needs. For details, write Charisma House Book Group, 600 Rinehart Road, Lake Mary, Florida 32746, or telephone (407) 333-0600.

UNFINISHED BUSINESS by David C. Cooper, DMin
Published by Charisma House
Charisma Media/Charisma House Book Group
600 Rinehart Road
Lake Mary, Florida 32746
www.charismahouse.com

Unless otherwise noted, all Scripture quotations are from the Holy Bible, New International Version. Copyright © 1973, 1978, 1984, International Bible Society. Used by permission.

Scripture quotations marked KJV are from the King James Version of the Bible.

Scripture quotations marked NAS are from the New American Standard Bible, copyright © 1960, 1962, 1963, 1968, 1971, 1972, 1973, 1975, 1977, 1995 by The Lockman Foundation. Used by permission. (www.Lockman.org)

Scripture quotations marked NLT are from the Holy Bible, New Living Translation, copyright © 1996, 2004, 2007. Used by permission of Tyndale House Publishers, Inc., Wheaton, IL 60189. All rights reserved.

Scripture quotations marked Phillips are from *The New Testament in Modern English*, Revised Edition. Copyright © 1958, 1960, 1972 by J. B. Phillips. Macmillan Publishing Co. Used by permission.

Cover design by Lisa Rae Cox
Design Director: Bill Johnson
Visit the author's website at www.davidcooper.org
Library of Congress Cataloging-in-Publication Data
Cooper, David C.
  Unfinished business / David Cooper, Dmin. -- First edition.
    pages cm
  Includes bibliographical references.
  ISBN 978-1-61638-870-6 (trade paper) -- ISBN 978-1-61638-871-3
(ebook)
  1. Regret--Religious aspects--Christianity. 2. Change (Psychology)-
-Religious aspects--Christianity. 3. Success--Religious aspects--
Christianity. I. Title.
  BV4909.C6785 2013
  248.4--dc23
                                          2013000443

First edition

13 14 15 16 17 — 987654321
Printed in the United States of America

This book is dedicated to my beautiful and faithful wife, Barbie, who has always believed in me and pushed me to move on to the next level.

CONTENTS

INTRODUCTION

THE NINETEENTH-CENTURY POET William Wordsworth wrote, "The Child is the father of the Man."[1] Those words are very true. No matter how long we live, we carry our childhoods with us. In a sense the past is always present with us. Our childhood experiences and memories continue to shape and influence us in the present in ways we often don't realize or understand. Everyone wants to live life to its fullest, but frequently the unfinished business of the past keeps us from living in the present.

We all have had experiences that left us with hurts, wounds, or regrets. But too many people are allowing pain from old wounds to rob them of hope for the future. We can't walk into a new season while clinging to the past. That old baggage will just pollute and destroy the new thing God wants to do.

When we experience pains and difficulties in life, Jesus wants us to "shake off the dust." That is what He taught His disciples to do when they went into towns and were rejected for their ministry: "If anyone will not welcome you or listen to your words, shake the dust off your feet when you leave that home or town" (Matt. 10:14). Still today Jesus's followers needed to know how to move on to the next opportunity without allowing the dust of the past to cling to them.

We will not be ready for the new until we shake off the old. We can never be ready for the new opportunity, the new challenge, the new life, the new blessing until we deal with our unfinished business. We must put off the dust of the old experiences of our lives or we will bring them into the new.

We tend to use the word *dust* figuratively. Expressions such as "bite the dust" or "wait until the dust settles" are a common part of our vocabulary. But in the Bible dust is associated with people. Adam was created from the dust of the ground (Gen. 2:7). The psalmist David says that God has compassion on us because He remembers that we are created from the dust (Ps. 103:13–14). When we die, our bodies return to the dust from which they came (Eccles. 12:7).

Science confirms that we are made of dust. Consider the miracle of human skin: one square inch of our skin contains 19 million cells, 625 sweat glands, 65 hairs, 19 feet of blood vessels, 19,000 sensory cells, and 20 microscopic animals called mites living on the surface. The body constantly sheds dead skin cells and replaces them with new ones. Seventy-five percent of dust in the average house is made up of dead skin cells.[2] Globally, dead skin accounts for about a billion tons of dust in the atmosphere. Your skin sheds 50,000 cells every minute.[3] (That brings a whole new meaning to spring cleaning!)

I like the story of the boy who listened attentively in church as his teacher explained how God had created Adam from the dust of the ground. The teacher went on to tell the kids that when we die, we return to the dust, quoting God's words to Adam: "From dust you have come, and to dust you will return." (See Genesis 3:19.) This fascinated the boy. Later that afternoon his mother found him on his knees looking under his bed at some dust that had gathered there. She got on her knees beside him and looked under the bed with him. "What are you looking at?" she asked. The boy said, "I don't know, but it's somebody who's either coming or going!"

That story always makes me laugh, but there is some truth in it. We truly are made of dust, and in more ways than one. If we hold on to the dust from the past, it becomes part of us, and if we don't learn to shake it off, as Jesus instructed His disciples to do, it will prevent us from moving forward in life. Our minds are so focused on what happened to us that we can't clearly see what is happening in the moment and what can happen if we open ourselves to a new work of God in our lives.

Many people talk about wanting something new in their lives. They want a new season. They want new relationships. They want new experiences. But often they're not ready for the new because they have unfinished business with the past. Until they recognize the dust they are carrying and learn to shake it off, the new won't work out for them. They'll end up ruining it with the dust from the past.

What kind of dust am I talking about? This unfinished business comes in many forms. There is the dust of anger, resentment, and hurt feelings. There is the dust of self-defeating labels, stereotypes, and prejudices. There is the dust of failures, poor decisions, and mistakes. There is the dust of perfectionism, poor self-image, and feelings of inadequacy. There is the dust of disappointment, unreached goals, and unfulfilled dreams. There is the dust of faulty attitudes, values, and beliefs that are contrary to God's will for our lives. There is the dust of deeply ingrained worry, fear, and anxiety.

We will never be ready for a new experience if we drag the old feelings with us. In this book you will learn not only how to identify the dust that's keeping you tied to the past but also how to shake it off so you can experience all that God has for you.

It's time to move forward. Do yourself a favor and allow the Holy Spirit to speak to you through the pages of this book.

Allow Him to reveal the unconscious attitudes and beliefs that have chained you to your past. Allow Him to speak to you about your unfinished business and break you through to a new way of thinking so you can live fully in the present.

Chapter 1

WATCH OUT FOR THAT ICEBERG!

Letting Go of Painful Memories

W E LIVE IN the computer age, but the greatest computer in the world is the human brain. Some have called the brain the most mysterious, intriguing organism of our universe. Weighing about three pounds, the brain contains some one hundred billion neurons, and each neuron is like a small computer. Over one hundred thousand chemical reactions occur in the brain every second, and the nerve cells send impulses to the body at the rate of two hundred miles per second. The brain stores ten trillion to fifteen trillion memories in a lifetime. Its left hemisphere controls logic, language, and mathematics. Its right hemisphere controls art, orientation to space, creativity, athletic coordination, mechanical abilities, and visual stimulation.[1]

The right brain controls the left side of the body and vice versa. Someone once observed that since the right brain controls the left side of the body, only left-handed people are in their right minds!

While the brain is a physical structure, the functions of the brain are referred to as the mind. The mind is the center of our intellect, will, and emotion; simply put, it is the way we think, feel, and act. Now here's what's interesting: the human mind is like an iceberg. The smallest part of an iceberg is above water level and can be seen. In much the same way, the information stored in our conscious mind is close to the surface of our thoughts and can be retrieved at will. The largest part of an iceberg is beneath water level and cannot be seen. Similarly our unconscious mind stores our every experience as well as everything we have ever learned, but we cannot always retrieve this information at will.

The television game show *Are You Smarter Than a Fifth Grader?* illustrates this truth. In the game adults attempt to answer questions from elementary school textbooks, which should be easy enough. The problem is that the information we learned in the fifth grade is stored in our unconscious mind, and we can't necessarily access it. We haven't really forgotten it; it has been stored away in a mental file—we just can't always get to the file. We know somewhere deep down which country the composer Mozart was born in, but we're just not sure whether it was Germany or Austria. (It was Austria.)

Sometimes when we go through painful experiences, especially during childhood, we repress those memories and the emotions attached to them in our unconscious mind so we don't have to deal with them. But the unconscious mind continues to influence and motivate us. Dreams are often a release of unresolved, repressed thoughts and feelings from the past. Thoughts and feelings we can't deal with at a conscious level are often processed at an unconscious level. Learning to confront the repressed thoughts and feelings of the past and to resolve and come to peace with them is vital to living fully in the present.

My best friend was killed in a head-on car crash in 1980, two years after we graduated from college. The Saturday morning when I received the news of his death still seems like only yesterday. I was numb when I learned he was gone, and I remained numb when I visited his family and was still numb when I attended his funeral. Even my wife, Barbie, asked me, "Why don't you cry?" I said, "I don't know. I just feel numb." But I would dream about my friend. And then I would wake up sobbing with overwhelming feelings of grief. I still dream about him. The feelings of grief gradually worked their way out in my dreams. While I wouldn't or couldn't deal with it in my conscious mind, the unconscious mind sought to resolve those feelings of sadness that had been repressed.

We don't have to live in the prison of repressed memories and feelings. We can shake off that dust and move on to a life that is full and free. We have to decide that carrying the dust of our past is not worth it and that whatever it takes, we're going to shake it off. We have to decide that life is too precious to waste in suffering with the unfinished business of the past.

Obviously we can't undo the negative and painful events we experienced—the past is over. But we can change our thinking about those things. We can shake off the dust of the painful memories—the thoughts, feelings, and attitudes that have become a deep-seated part of our minds because of the pain and hurt we endured.

We can't change the past, but we can change our perspective of the past. It has been said that perception is reality. Perspective is power. Psychologist Albert Ellis developed a counseling model called rational emotive behavior therapy.[2] I've outlined it below:

A + B = C

Problem + Perception = Pain

According to Ellis, it's our faulty beliefs that cause our emotional pain, not the actual problems of life. It's the problem plus our perspective that determines our emotions. We can't control the problems of life, and we can't control our feelings, but we can control our thoughts. Life's circumstances don't determine how we feel. It's how we think about our circumstances that determine how we feel.

Our feelings are subject to our thinking. If we think negative thoughts in response to our problems, we will experience negative feelings. If we think positive thoughts, we will experience positive feelings. We make the choice between victory and defeat by the way we react to the situations of life. If we respond to our problems and our suffering with the wrong perspective—with anger, resentment, self-pity, or discouragement, for example— we will feel emotional pain. If we respond with faith, hope, love, forgiveness, and confidence, we will feel perfect peace. If we change our minds, we will change our lives.

This is true even of the most painful experiences of neglect, abuse, and injustice. We have to acknowledge the things that have happened to us and face the feelings that result from them. We have to confront the pain that others have caused us rather than telling ourselves that the traumatic events didn't occur. But after we squarely acknowledge our painful memories, we can choose how we think about those experiences. We can choose to release the thoughts of anger, low self-esteem, self-blame, guilt, shame, embarrassment, resentment, and fear. The day we decide that the painful events of our lives do not define or determine who we are—whether we caused those events or someone else hurt us—then we are on our way to freedom.

Corrie ten Boom, survivor of Hitler's death camps, learned how to master her mind in the worst of circumstances. In her autobiography *Tramp for the Lord* she shared this anonymous poem that helped her put her pain into perspective:

> My life is but a weaving, between my God and me.
> I do not choose the colors, He worketh steadily,
> Oftimes He weaveth sorrow, and I in foolish pride,
> Forget He sees the upper, and I the under side.
> Not till the loom is silent, and the shuttles cease to fly,
> Will God unroll the canvas and explain the reason
>   why.
> The dark threads are as needful in the skillful
>   Weaver's hand,
> As the threads of gold and silver in the pattern He has
>   planned.[3]

FACE THE FACTS

So how can we shake off the dust of painful memories and repressed feelings? First, we need to recognize the dust that we are carrying. We can only change the things in our lives that we are aware of. We can't shake off the dust unless we know that we have it. Paul the apostle said, "Examine yourselves...test yourselves" (2 Cor. 13:5). Socrates said, "The unexamined life is not worth living."[4] It's hard to face up to some of our baggage, but doing so is our first step to being free.

The Bible puts it another way: "Let us throw off everything that hinders and the sin that so easily entangles, and let us run with perseverance the race marked out for us" (Heb. 12:1). We can't run the race of life, of marriage, of raising our children, or of building a career until we throw aside every weight: the emotional stress, pain, and scars that we carry. A runner has to dress lightly, and we need to live lightly, not weighed down with fear, resentment, or failure. These weights become "dust" in our lives, and Jesus wants us to shake them off before we go on to the next season of life.

It's hard for us to face up to the dust that we are carrying or the weights that entangle us. Many people never get over their emotional issues because they don't want to face up to them. They live in denial. They get defensive when someone tries to help them face up to things. We would do better if we were less defensive and more open to seeing ourselves and owning our personal issues. There is no reason for us to feel embarrassed or ashamed because of what we feel. None of us are any different from anyone else. All of us have feelings, thoughts, and behaviors that weigh us down and keep us from living our best life possible.

One of my favorite scriptures on faith is about Abraham: "Without weakening in his faith, he faced the fact that his body was as good as dead.... Yet he did not waver through unbelief regarding the promise of God" (Rom. 4:19–20). Abraham had great faith even while he faced the facts. So much of what is called faith today is not faith; it's fantasy thinking and denial of reality. We have to learn to face the facts about our situations, our relationships, and ourselves if we expect to experience the promises of God and see real changes in our lives. Many times we deal with only surface issues, or symptoms, instead of the real issues and root causes of our personal struggles and troubled relationships.

Here are some common ways we hide our feelings and avoid real issues:

+ We stay busy with projects or hobbies.

+ We avoid meaningful conversations about our feelings.

+ We pretend that something hasn't happened.

+ We use substances to cope with or to mask our feelings.

+ We compulsively exercise or engage in other compulsive behaviors.

+ We escape through excessive TV watching or reading.

+ We overwork.

+ We harbor anger under the cover of peace.

+ We tell ourselves that we shouldn't feel a certain way.

+ We intellectualize, analyze, and justify feelings.

+ We observe religious routines instead of nurturing a close relationship with God.

+ We keep relationships surface to avoid intimacy and transparency.

I recently went to my doctor for a physical exam. The office ran all the basic tests on me. When they called me with test results about my heart rate, cholesterol level, and lung x-rays, I didn't get defensive and say, "That's not right. Run the test again. There's no way I could have that problem!" No, I accepted the results (which, fortunately, were great) as facts. We have to learn to accept the emotional and personal facts about ourselves just as we do the physical ones if we are going to move past the hurts and disappointments we have experienced. There is always a new season for us, but we have to shake off the dust to experience and enjoy it. We don't have to continue to feel anxiety, hurt, or pain. But we have to be willing to face those things so that we can decide to shake them off.

WHAT ARE YOU FEELING RIGHT NOW?

Many people are blind to their feelings. I often help people in counseling to recognize their feelings and to identify them. When I ask, "What are you feeling right now?" or "How did you feel when that happened to you?", they usually answer by telling me what they think rather than what they feel. They say: "I am confused." "That person wouldn't listen to me." "They were wrong in what they did." But I point out to them that those are thoughts, not feelings. It's much easier to talk about what we think than how we feel. But it's important that we understand how we feel about the things that have happened to us in the past, because those feelings affect the present, even though we may be unaware of it.

Our feelings are the deepest and truest expression of who we really are. Talking about our feelings makes us feel exposed and vulnerable. That's why we are guarded, afraid to express our true selves and our true feelings, thinking that people won't accept us for who we really are. We think people will judge us, so we hide our feelings from them and even from ourselves.

I give people "feeling words" to help them start talking about their emotions, words such as *love, happy, angry, frustrated, resentful, mad, depressed, hopeful*. I ask them to complete the sentence, "I feel…" Still, so many people say, "It's hard for me to talk about my feelings." Or, "I have never really been in touch with my feelings or shared them with anyone." Their comments reflect how typical it is for us to walk around with pent-up negative feelings that sabotage our relationships and our goals. This pain from the past keeps us from enjoying new opportunities and can even prevent us from *having* new opportunities.

If we go out to eat and, perhaps, get mustard on our chin, and a friend discreetly points to her chin, we quickly grab a napkin, wipe off the mustard, and thank our friend. But if the same person points out to us our feelings of anger or our controlling behavior or our negative attitude, we get defensive. The people closest to us wouldn't tell us that we had problems in our lives—dust that we need to shake off—if we didn't have them.

We need to be as receptive to feedback from others about the emotional and spiritual baggage we are carrying as we are when someone discreetly tells us that we have mustard on our chin. We don't want to sit through a meal looking foolish, and we don't want to go through life with issues from the past that keeps us from living full lives in the present. Before we can shake off the emotional and spiritual dust of our past, we have to become aware of it and to accept it as real.

It's Not Worth It

Once we start facing our feelings of pain, we have to decide to deal with them. We can only shake off the dust from our lives when we decide that the dust is not worth carrying. We need to be good managers of our lives, and the unfinished business of the past keeps us from living the best life we can live. Harboring unresolved anger, resentment, fear, and disappointment is not worth the toll it takes on us mentally, emotionally, physically, and relationally. Conversations with our friends in which we rehash the past and get more and more upset are a waste of the mental and emotional energy we need for today.

Repressed feelings make us feel fatigued and depressed. Feelings need to be felt, shared, and expressed—not bottled up.

We may bury our feelings and deny them, but they continue to affect us: We blow up over small issues. We have trouble sleeping. We experience stress and physical symptoms such as ulcers. We have sleep disturbances and bad dreams. We are edgy with others. We shut down emotionally and keep our distance in relationships.

Long-term repressed emotions can also be linked to physical illness, chronic fatigue, arthritis, and many other health problems. Repressed emotions affect our behavior and our reactions to our current circumstances. They keep us stuck in past events and prevent us from living in the present. Repressed childhood feelings wound us psychologically and even shape the way we see ourselves and the way we relate to others. We often carry our childhood fears and insecurities with us throughout life, unless we see the dust they cause and shake it off.

We repress our memories and our feelings to defend ourselves against pain or anxiety. We do it as a survival instinct emotionally. But the repressed material continues to affect us and to influence the way we think, feel, and act. Sometimes we are confused about what motivates us and causes us to act and respond the way we do. Even the apostle Paul said, "I do not understand what I do. For what I want to do I do not do, but what I hate I do" (Rom. 7:15). Paul felt the polar forces at work within his unconscious mind. He too didn't understand why he acted in ways that were contradictory to his highest goals and purest ambitions to be all that God had created him to be.

The fact is, some experiences are so painful and hurtful that we don't have the understanding or the ability to deal with them. Once we bury them in the unconscious, we can actually even forget those things happened to us. Over time we can lose all memory of certain painful experiences and the feelings associated with them. This is a basic defense mechanism that helps us avoid great pain. But no matter how much we hide from our pain, we can't avoid its effects. Carrying emotional and spiritual dust is not worth it!

A New Season Is Coming

I live in Georgia. I grew up in Atlanta and have spent most of my life here. One of the things I love most about Georgia is the changing of the seasons. We have four distinct seasons. Just around the time I get bored with spring, summer arrives. When I am tired of the heat, the winds of autumn start to blow gently. Then comes the cold with just enough snow to enjoy but not enough to shut the city down. When I'm tired of freezing, the flowers and trees start to bloom, and the beauty of spring unfolds again.

Seasons are wonderful times of change. They signal the end of the old and the beginning of the new. When we're tired of one season, it's great to know that there's a new one on the way. Seasons give us something to look forward to. If you are in a difficult season right now, bogged down with the pain of the past, know that you can shake off that dust and go on to a new beginning.

Jesus told His disciples to shake off the dust of any town in which they were rejected so they could go on to the next town. But shaking off the dust is only half the equation; we have to go on to the next season. God always has a new season, a new assignment, and a new opportunity for us, and we have to believe that truth if we truly want to shake off the dust.

Don't stay in the place of your hurt and disappointment trying to fix it or resolve it—shake it off! And don't get stuck in between shaking off the dust and experiencing a new season.

When you see the dust you've been carrying and you shake it off, then complete the journey by going on to experience a new season. Shake off the dust and be on your way to a new season!

A schoolteacher came to see me for counseling. She was depressed and angry because she was being demoted instead of promoted by her school administrator. Even though she had taught for several years and had seniority over other teachers, the administrator wanted her to take the class of students with behavioral disorders. Although the school administrator told her she was being placed over the class because she was the most qualified, she felt she was being patronized. This woman appealed the decision, but the school administrator's decision was final.

She talked to me about changing careers, even though her life's goal was to be a teacher. She looked into changing schools, but there were no openings. She felt trapped in her situation. I suggested to her that maybe this was a great opportunity for her to bless the kids who would be in the class and that maybe the administrator had chosen her because she really was the most qualified. She quickly dismissed that idea.

She came to see me a second time, and her depression and anger hadn't changed. Again I suggested that maybe this was a great opportunity for her and that maybe God was even opening a door for her to bless these kids who needed her teaching gifts.

When she returned to see me for a third visit, she was a totally different person. She was full of joy and excitement when she walked into my office. "What happened to you?" I asked.

"I started thinking about what you said—that maybe this was an open door of opportunity for me," she replied. "So I went over to the school and stood in the classroom to envision the children who would be in the new class. I prayed that God would give me the ability to teach and encourage them. I have made the classroom my own by redecorating everything in it. I can now see the students in my mind. I am no longer afraid of the challenge, but I have embraced it as God's call on my life."

Now, nothing had changed in the world around this woman, but she was excited because the world within her had changed. Her world of thoughts and attitudes changed from depression, anger, and fear to joy, faith, and anticipation. The quality of our lives never rises above the level of our thinking. Once this woman's thinking changed about that class, her feelings changed.

So how did the story end? Well, the woman started teaching the class, and I saw her after the first quarter was over. She was so excited about what had taken place in the lives of the children that she told me, "I have requested that the school allow me to keep teaching the class of students with behavioral disorders." What had been a problem was now her purpose. What had been an administrative mistake was now her appointed mission. What had made her depressed now made her happy! Why? Because she mastered her mind, changed her perspective, and embraced a new season as an opportunity rather than as an obstacle. We often stumble over the thing we should step up on to take us to a new level.

Once this woman shook off the dust of disappointment, anger, fear, and the hopeless feeling of being trapped, she found new purpose and happiness in her career. Many times the answer for us in our struggles is not to change the world around us but to change the world within us.

Chapter 2

DON'T GET OVER IT—
GET ON WITH IT!

Moving Beyond the Past

M Y PHONE RANG late one Christmas evening. The
woman on the other end of the line was distraught.
Her husband had died about six months earlier. She
and I had talked on several occasions as I tried to help her work
through the grieving process, but she was stuck in her sorrow
and depression.

"How can I ever get over Ray's death?" she cried. "I'm so
alone. I've got nothing left to live for. How can I get over it?"

Suddenly, although I was half asleep, a thought popped into
my head, and I blurted out, "Don't get over it—get on with it!"

My words hit her like a ton of bricks. She stopped crying,
got quiet, and regained her composure. There was an awkward
moment of silence. Then she asked, "What do you mean—get
on with it?"

I thought to myself, "What *do* I mean?"

I told her that she would always love her husband and would
always miss him. No one could take away the pain and loss she
felt. "Your pain," I said, "is the measure of your love.

"Stop trying to get over Ray's death," I told her. "There are some things in life we never get over, and this is one of them. But," I continued, "you can get on with it.

"Keep your pain tucked away in your heart. Treasure your memories of Ray forever. But begin to live the rest of your life despite your pain."

After our conversation, and several subsequent ones, this lady began to understand the principle: *Don't get over it—get on with!* And she started to get on with it. She started to dream again. Over the next few weeks she thought about:

+ Places to travel

+ Career opportunities

+ New skills to develop

+ Educational challenges

+ Volunteer opportunities

+ Charitable work

+ A new place to live

She rose to meet the challenge of getting on with life even when it hurt. There are some things in life that are so painful that we'll never get over them. The good news is, we don't have to. We can always get on with it even when we can't get over it. Will Rogers said, "Even if you are on the right track, you'll get run over if you just sit there."[1]

Make Your Past an Asset, Not a Liability

Do you ever wish life had an "undo" feature the way a computer does? Wouldn't it be great if we could just hit "undo" and travel back in time to correct mistakes we have made, take back misspoken words, and change everything we regret? I would change a lot of things, as I'm sure you would. Unfortunately, life doesn't come with a button like that.

Our memories of missed opportunities, personal failures, and poor decisions can form a prison, locking us in the past and out of the present. We can romanticize the past as we relish in the glory of days gone by. While we are definitely influenced by the past, we don't have to get stuck in it. The past should be an asset, not a liability.

Some people drag the past around the way Linus in the cartoon *Peanuts* dragged his blanket with him everywhere he went. These people are always dealing with the past in one way or another. They're preoccupied with getting over the past, forgetting the past, working through the past, and so forth.

Here's the problem: every minute spent working on the past is another minute lost to the present moment. The present is on standby when we live in the past. Sure, there are legitimate issues for us to deal with from our past. But addressing these things needs to be done intentionally and with the goal of moving beyond the past. The only way our past can become an asset is for us to use it as a teacher. The past becomes an asset when we use it as a springboard to launch us into the future.

We tend to make a bigger deal about the influence of the past than we should. But our thoughts, feelings, and actions are not always due to the past. When we think they are, it leads us down the path of blaming the past instead of taking charge of the present.

The logic goes that to understand ourselves, we have to explore our past and then resolve it, often through therapy or inner healing. There's nothing wrong with analyzing the past—it is important up to a point. But even if we understood everything about our past, it wouldn't change the present. For us to change, action is required. We have to set goals and implement a plan of action. Analysis is important because it helps us understand ourselves better, but at some point we need to move from analysis to action.

The past no longer exists. We can't go back and relive it, but here are some things we can do with it. We can:

+ Be thankful for the past

+ Regret the past

+ Grieve over the past

+ Live in the past

+ Learn from the past

+ Romanticize the past

+ Forget the past

+ Blame the past

+ Celebrate the past

The one thing we can't do is *change the past*. Say it aloud to yourself right now: "I can't change the past!"

Since we can change only the present, we need to focus our energy on the here and now. Life doesn't come with an undo command. You and I can't turn back the hands of time. We waste valuable time when we obsess over the past. Life is right now. *Now!* The key to getting beyond your past is to make the most of the moment.

Your life, like mine, holds a mixture of good and bad experiences, successes and failures, pain and pleasure. In the equation of who we are, our pain is just as important as our positive experiences. So don't be ashamed of your past or embarrassed by your past, and don't deny your past. Make it an asset instead of a liability by learning from it. Yesterday can make you a better person today if you use it wisely.

Pushed or Pulled?

The past is only one piece of the puzzle to understanding ourselves. The future affects us too. The past pushes us, but the future pulls us. Many people feel that their past experiences, their childhood, and their upbringing are the only factors that shape who they are. They feel as though the past pushes them around in the sense that their past determines who they are today. They often seek to explain their present issues by talking about what happened to them in the past, almost assuming that the reason they think, feel, or act a certain way today is because of what happened to them in the past.

On the other hand, we can set new goals for ourselves that will pull us out of where we are today and lead us to a new place in our lives. In this sense the future pulls us forward to becoming the person we want to be. You are just as influenced by your future goals as you are by your past experiences. Sometimes the reason life is not working for you today is not something in your past but rather the lack of future goals. Without goals to pull you forward, you will stay stuck where you are. But you're not stuck because of what happened to you yesterday; you're stuck because you don't have clear-cut future goals to propel you forward in life.

All our behaviors have a goal. In other words, we behave certain ways in order to gain something. If we want to understand ourselves better, we need to take a close look at our goals—our desires. Instead of asking ourselves, "What happened to me in the past?", we should ask, "What will I gain for my future by acting this way?" Such a question keeps our focus on the present, and that is all we have control over.

Even dysfunctional behaviors—addictions, poor communication patterns, and emotional outbursts—are carried out because of what we expect to achieve out of them: the high or feeling of control or temporary reprieve from the pressures of life. All our behavior is rooted in what we hope to get out of it.

Unraveling the mysterious *why* of our actions has more to do with the present than it does with the past. It takes serious reflection and insight, and the process of understanding the goals of our behaviors, especially our dysfunctional ones, is greatly helped by professional counseling. But we can usually discover which goals we are trying to reach simply by taking an honest look at ourselves.

Our goals are often unconscious. We are unaware of why we do what we do and why we feel the way we feel. Deeply ingrained behaviors, both positive and negative, become part of us because over the course of time, these actions have been rewarded. They've produced some kind of payoff, so we continue to act in the same way.

Think about the alcoholic. He continues to drink even though it brings him nothing but problems, because there is a payoff. He's getting something out of it—otherwise he would stop. Maybe he likes the feeling of being free from pressure or the mental escape that alcohol brings.

It's important to understand that he doesn't drink because his parents did. He may have learned the behavior at home, but that's not *why* he drinks. Blaming parents for alcoholic practices is an excuse that keeps people from taking charge of their lives.

There are just as many people from alcoholic homes who refuse to drink as there are those who become alcoholics.

Some people are more prone to addictions than others are, but drinking is still a matter of choice. Substance abusers have to understand what motivates their addictions—what they are getting out of them—in order to make a new choice and take control of their addiction. We are always free to choose how we want to live, regardless of our past. When we know this truth, we are ready to cut ties with the past and start living in the present.

Consider the verbally abusive man. He doesn't abuse others simply because he grew up in an abusive home or because he's under too much stress. He abuses for a reason. Most likely abusing others gives him the feeling of being superior or of being in control. He needs to dominate, so he flexes his muscle by intimidating others at home, at work, at church, and in social settings. He may blame his upbringing, and that may certainly be where he saw abusive language modeled, but that's not why he's abusive. Not everyone who grows up in an abusive home becomes abusive.

Abusers become worse when their victims submit to their treatment, because the submission is a form of reward. The goal of abuse is to get the other person to submit. When the victim submits, the abuser wins, and the bad behavior is reinforced. The truth is, the abuser is responsible for his own actions. Once he faces his responsibility and gives up the goal of being in control, he is on his way to stopping the abusive behavior. The past may help explain the present, but it is not an excuse for the present.

Consider the rebellious child. We don't say, "Well, the kid must have had some traumatic experience while she was still in her mother's womb." No, we don't focus so much on the past in order to understand rebellion in children. Again, we look at the present. What is the child trying to accomplish by being rebellious? What are her goals? Perhaps she is trying to get attention, or maybe she is seeking to control the family by acting out, or possibly she is even punishing her parents by being disruptive. She rebels for a reason. As soon as the parents know what the child wants, they can help her reach her goal in a constructive way.

The Past Is Resolved When the Present Is Fulfilled

Take hold of this principle: *the past is resolved when the present is fulfilled.* When we are happy, we don't waste time analyzing our past. We're too busy enjoying life. It's only when life comes to a grinding halt and we lose our sense of fulfillment that we become preoccupied with the past.

Stop asking, "How can I get over my past?", and start asking, "How can I get on with my life?" Change your goal from trying to resolve the past to being fulfilled in the present. Quit wasting so much time and energy getting over the past. Use what's happened in the past to move on in the present. We can't drive a car by looking through the rearview mirror, and we can't live our lives fully today by looking at the past.

Remember when the Israelites were trapped in the desert after they had been delivered from Egypt? They were in a jam. Pharaoh's army was pursuing them from behind. The Red Sea was in front of them. The people complained to Moses, "It would have been better for us to have stayed in Egypt than to die out here in the desert!"

The people cried out to the Lord, and "the LORD said to

Moses, 'Why are you crying out to me? Tell the Israelites to move on'" (Exod. 14:15). That's exactly what God is saying to you and to me when we're stuck in the past and paralyzed by fear, resentment, failure, tragedy, or disappointment: "*Move on!*"

Let me show you this powerful truth in Scripture: "But one thing I do: Forgetting what is behind and straining toward what is ahead, I press on toward the goal to win the prize for which God has called me heavenward in Christ Jesus" (Phil. 3:13–14). If you want to shake off the dust of the past, adopt this statement as your life mission. Everybody needs a personal mission statement for his life, and this is a great one. Regardless of what has happened in the past, it is possible to be fulfilled in the present with the attitude, "I press on!"

The apostle Paul says he strains for what lies ahead. Consider the phrase "what lies ahead" (NAS). Do you have a clear-cut vision of who you want to be and what you want to accomplish with your life? We can't strain for what lies ahead until we *see* what lies ahead. We can't get our minds off the past until we can see something better for ourselves in the future. Once we get our focus on the future, our present will be fulfilled, and we will automatically stop dwelling on the past.

Young people need a vision for their future. They need a creed to believe, a song to sing, and a cause greater than themselves for which to live. This is what Paul meant when he said, "For to me, to live is Christ" (Phil. 1:21).

How would you complete this sentence: For to me, to live is _____. What would you write in that blank as your ultimate purpose in life?

We need purpose in order to find fulfillment in life. There has to be a *why* in life, not just a *what*. Why do you do what you do? What is the *why* that gives your life purpose? Author

H. G. Wells said, "Until a man has found God, he begins at no beginning and works to no end."[2] Knowing Jesus Christ as our Savior gives us purpose. When we know Him, honoring Him and sharing Him with others become the great motive of our lives. We live for Him and not just for ourselves.

Once we see where we are going, we can then strain for what lies ahead, as the apostle Paul wrote in Philippians 3:13. The word *strain* is an athletic term that describes how Olympic runners stretch out with all their energy to cross the finish line and win the prize. The runners lunge forward, stretching out their bodies to cross the tape with all the energy they can muster.

Take a look at your own life. What lies ahead for you? What is your dream? What are you living for? Whom are you living for? What is your vision for your life? What do you want to achieve? Where do you want to go? What do you want to experience? These are the questions that form the most important goals of our lives. Without meaningful goals we flounder in life. Now is the time for us to get a clear sense of direction for what we want to do with our lives and to go for it with all our might.

The apostle Paul had a sense of destiny. He wrote, "I press on to take hold of that for which Christ Jesus took hold of me" (Phil. 3:12). He believed that Jesus had taken hold of his life for a high and holy purpose. God "takes hold" of every person for a higher purpose than just to live an average existence. Many people today are asking what it means to be a Christian. Some even describe the Christian experience as "finding the Lord." The truth is, the Lord finds us! He takes hold of us to save us from our sins and give us a new life. Jesus Christ took hold of you when you came to know Him. He seized possession of your life that He might use you and work through you for His glory. You have a divine destiny. Now go for it!

The purpose of God for our lives will not become a reality passively. We have to take action to embrace God's purpose. His purpose requires our participation. God does not manipulate us as if we were figures on a chessboard; He works in partnership with us. Many people are too passive in their pursuits. Some view the blessings of God as some kind of divine luck that arbitrarily makes some people successful while the rest of us struggle through life. God's blessings are not random. His blessings follow faith, obedience, and perseverance. If we are going to shake off the dust of the past, we have to strain for what lies ahead. We can't expect the promise of what lies ahead to happen by itself. Life is not what happens to us; it's what we make happen.

America is plagued by a "path of least resistance" mentality. A few years ago the phrase "the dumbing down of America" was used to describe the demise of our country's educational system. Instead of providing higher education, we lowered the academic standards. We have often catered to the least common denominator instead of raising ourselves up to a high standard.

Athletics has eliminated the concept of losing so that everyone can be a winner, as if losing would damage a child's psyche. Losing happens to be fundamental to developing the qualities of determination and perseverance that are needed for achieving success. Everyone needs to experience the pain of losing so they can appreciate the joy of victory. The treacherous climb to the top of the mountain, the long journey through the hot desert sands, and the hard knocks experienced through endless trial and error are necessary ingredients for reaching our highest potential.

I remember getting fired from a summer job I had when I was a teenager. Looking back, it was a great experience because it made me appreciate my next job more. I think everyone should be fired at least once. It changes our attitude toward work and life's opportunities and makes us work harder. Loss can provide us with a perfect opportunity to use our past to fulfill our present.

Oswald Chambers writes in *My Utmost for His Highest*: "God does not give us overcoming life—He gives us life as we overcome. The strain of life is what builds our strength. If there is no strain, there will be no strength. Are you asking God to give you life, liberty, and joy? He cannot, unless you are willing to accept the strain."[3]

No pain, no gain. Paul the apostle said, "I strain for what lies ahead." The only way we make it to our desired destination is to strain to reach our goals with all the determination and energy we possess.

+ Strain to do God's will
+ Strain to have a good marriage
+ Strain to build a happy home
+ Strain to get your education
+ Strain to achieve financial success
+ Strain to release your potential
+ Strain for that which lies ahead

Where You're Going Is More Important Than Where You've Been

Our lives are ahead of us, not behind us. When Israel faced the challenges of the wilderness, they kept looking back to the comforts of Egypt. All they got for looking back was forty years in the desert—not just in the desert but *wandering* in the desert. We have two choices: we can wander in life or we can pursue our dreams.

If we don't take charge of our future, we will wander our way through life—and get nowhere. Focusing on the past makes us wander in the present and miss our future promise. We will miss our promised land if we don't learn to look ahead of us instead of behind us. The answer for us is not to go back but to go forward.

I once read a quote that said if you are not actively pursuing the person you want to be, you are pursuing the person you don't want to be. Shake off the dust of the past. Open your eyes to see what lies ahead, and strain for it with all the passion and determination you have. Every step you take toward your future is one step farther from your past. Soon whatever has troubled you will become a distant memory.

Chapter 3

FORGETFUL AND FRUITFUL

Rising Above Hurt

I N Lewis Carroll's *Through the Looking Glass* the white knight tries to anticipate all the problems that might await him on a journey. To protect his horse from shark bites, the knight attaches anklets to its legs. To guard against the ridiculous idea that a mouse might run down the horse's back, the knight keeps a mousetrap on the horse's side. He attempts to prepare for every possible need, but with so many cumbersome things attached to the horse, every time it stops (which the horse did often), the knight falls right on his head![1]

So it is with us. We try everything we can to protect ourselves from the pains of life, but eventually we get hurt. And most of the time hurt comes from conflict in our relationships with others.

John Donne wrote, "No man is an island, entire of itself."[2] Our level of peace and happiness is based mainly on our relationships. If our relationships are in order, we are usually happy. But if we have conflict with the people in our lives, we can't move forward in a healthy way until we get things resolved.

Who we are—our personality, character, and temperament—are shaped by our closest relationships. Our purpose for living is based largely on our relationships and on the people who are dependent upon us.

God created us for relationships. The first thing He said about Adam was, "It is not good for the man to be alone" (Gen. 2:18). Or maybe the first thing He said was, "I can do better than that." So He created Eve! In either case, He made a partner for Adam, and the human story began with a relationship.

Jesus summed up real spirituality in terms of relationships. He said that the entire law and the prophets hang on two commandments: love the Lord your God, and love your neighbor as yourself. (See Matthew 22:37–40.)

The price of close relationships is to take the risk of getting hurt. If we love deeply, we will at times be hurt deeply. The only way to never get hurt is to avoid close relationships. But then we live lonely lives. So we are going to get hurt by others. The question is, how can we shake off the dust of hurt that we have experienced and be willing to get close again to others?

We don't like to admit we are hurt. We put up our defenses, and like turtles, we draw into our shells to protect ourselves. The story of Joseph teaches us how to handle hurt so that we become better, not bitter.

I don't know of anyone who went through more hurt in his family relationships. Joseph's older brothers hated him and were jealous of him because their father, Jacob, treated Joseph with special favor. It's always a mistake to show favoritism— and Jacob went overboard in showing favor toward Joseph. He gave him expensive clothes that were always a reminder to his brothers that Joseph was the favored son.

Joseph also had a dream from God. In that dream he saw himself in a great position of leadership, with his brothers bowing down to him. He made the mistake of sharing his dream with his family. His brothers were insulted and angry, and they accused Joseph of being full of pride in thinking that he was going to be in charge of them.

The grudge they nursed toward him grew worse. The older brothers decided it was time to get rid of Joseph. At first they thought of murdering him and telling their father that a wild animal had killed him. Not having the stomach for murder, they sold him as a slave to traveling gypsies who ended up taking him to Egypt and selling him there as a servant to Potiphar, an official with the government.

The brothers kept Joseph's expensive, ornamental coat that their father had made especially for him and covered it with an animal's blood. They showed it to their father and told him that Joseph had been killed and devoured by a wild animal. Jacob went into deep depression, lost all joy in life, and was never the same after the news of his son's death.

Now Joseph was only seventeen years old when this tragedy happened to him. In Egypt he began his work as a servant in Potiphar's household. One day Potiphar's wife tried to seduce Joseph. When he resisted her advances, she became angry and accused him of attempted rape. Potiphar obviously believed his wife over Joseph. As a result, Joseph was arrested and sentenced to life in prison.

Joseph would spend the next twelve years of his life in prison as an innocent man. He lost his family, his young-adult years, and his opportunities—in short, he lost everything because of the jealousy of his brothers. Furthermore, where was God? God had given him a dream! Where was that dream now? Not only was Joseph not in charge as he had seen in his dream, but also he was a prisoner! How could God let this happen to him?

But Joseph did not choose to be bitter toward God or his

family. That's the remarkable part of the story. While he lost everything around him, he never lost his faith within. It's what's within us, not what's around us, that makes or breaks us.

After twelve years of imprisonment Joseph got a break—not a jailbreak but a grace break! Joseph was taken to Pharaoh to interpret the leader's troubling dream. Joseph told Pharaoh that his dream meant that Egypt would have seven years of booming prosperity followed by seven years of drought and an economic depression. Pharaoh was shocked, and he asked Joseph what he should do. God gave Joseph a plan that would save Egypt's economy, and overnight Joseph went from the prison to the palace! He was appointed second in command to Pharaoh himself, and he held that high political position for the rest of his life. When God acts on our behalf, He can turn any situation around in a heartbeat.

Joseph was married to the daughter of an Egyptian priest, and he and his wife had two sons. Now get this: the names Joseph gave his boys tell us everything about the winning attitude of this man. Joseph named one of his sons Manasseh, saying, "God has made me forget all my trouble and all my father's household," and the other Ephraim, saying, "God has made me fruitful in the land of my suffering" (Gen. 41:51–52). Amazing! In everything he had suffered and despite the hurt his family had brought him, Joseph said God had made him forgetful and fruitful! (See Genesis 37–41.)

FLYING HIGH OR LIVING LOW?

There are two facts of life in Joseph's story: it is a story of a man's ability to transcend his situation, and it is a story about God's power and promise to restore what we have lost. The word *transcend* means "to rise above" or to "extend notably beyond ordinary limits."[3] The way an eagle rises toward the sun and above everything that threatens it on the ground is the way God wants us to rise above our hurts. We don't have to live a low-level life. We don't have to strike back when someone hurts us. We don't have to repay evil for evil. We can repay good for evil, blessing for cursing, and forgiveness for insult if we choose to rise above it all and live on a higher plane.

Have you ever thought about Isaiah 40:31 in that light? Look at it: "Those who hope in the LORD will renew their strength. They will soar on wings like eagles." What do eagles do when life gets tough? They fly high. They rise above, and so should we. That's what Joseph did. His brothers lived low-level lives of bitterness, hatred, and jealousy. Joseph flew high on eagles' wings with faith, forgiveness, and peace.

We have the power to live on a higher plane than the people who have hurt us do. The solution for us is not to attack, correct, or judge them. The answer is to rise above the hurt and to put our faith in God to provide for us, regardless of how we have been hurt by others.

Joseph transcended his hurt, and that opened the way for God to restore everything he had lost. It was in Egypt that Joseph experienced the God of restoration. To restore means "to put or bring back into existence or use; to bring back to or put back into a former or original state; to put again in possession of something."[4] David said, "He restores my soul" (Ps. 23:3), and he prayed, "Restore to me the joy of your salvation" (Ps. 51:12). God promises us:

> "I will restore you to health and heal your wounds,"
> declares the LORD, "because you are called an out-
> cast, Zion for whom no one cares." This is what the

> LORD says: "I will restore the fortunes of Jacob's tents and have compassion on his dwellings; the city will be rebuilt on her ruins, and the palace will stand in its proper place. From them will come songs of thanksgiving and the sound of rejoicing."
>
> —JEREMIAH 30:17–19

The prophet Nahum said, "The LORD will restore the splendor of Jacob like the splendor of Israel, though destroyers have laid them waste and have ruined their vines" (Nah. 2:2). God promises, "I will repay you for the years the locusts have eaten…You will have plenty to eat, until you are full, and you will praise the name of the LORD your God" (Joel 2:25–26). God says, "I am making everything new!" (Rev. 21:5). God has given us the ministry of restoration.

We may have suffered great hurt, but getting even is not the answer. Getting even means going down to the low level of the people who have hurt us. The answer is to rise above the hurt and to live on the higher plane of faith and forgiveness. If we try to fight our own battles, we will make a bigger mess of our relationships and experience greater ruin. If we rise above the hurt, we will see God restore what we have lost.

You may be asking, "How can I fly high and overcome my hurt?" Look at what Joseph did and follow his formula. He said, "God made me forget and made me fruitful." God gave Joseph the ability to forget his hurt and to be fruitful, even in a land of suffering. God will give us the same ability, but we also have to begin to forget and be fruitful.

God Can Do What You Can't Do

You may be saying to yourself, "I can't forget the bad things that have happened to me. I can't let go of them. I'm too hurt by what people have done to me." You are right—you can't let go! But God can! Joseph named his first son Manasseh, which means, "God has made me forget all my trouble and my father's household" (Gen. 41:51). Joseph didn't say he forgot the hurt by himself. He said God had made him forget.

Joseph had to forget two specific sources of hurt: his painful circumstances and his painful family history. Forgetting these things did not mean he couldn't recollect the past. It means he could remember them without resenting his family. As Joseph thought about his childhood and his family, he was not crippled by feelings of anger, depression, and grief over what had been lost. Neither would he spend the rest of his life trying to fix his dysfunctional family. He went on to have his own family.

This old English riddle, which later became a nursery rhyme, expresses this truth:

> Humpty Dumpty sat on a wall.
> Humpty Dumpty had a great fall.
> All the king's horses and all the king's men,
> Couldn't put Humpty together again.

Humpty Dumpty is depicted in the riddle as an egg. When he fell from his high and lofty position, he was shattered into pieces. All the resources at his disposal could not restore him. So it is with life. We experience seasons in which our dreams are shattered and we can't put our world back together again, no matter how hard we try. Learning to accept the fact that life moves on and that we can't return to a former season in life to relive it is important in handling life.

While we can't always put life back together the way it was, we can always build a new life. That's the power of the only three things that last in this life: faith, hope, and love. Faith helps us believe that a new life is possible. Hope helps us see a clear vision of that new life. And love enables us to forgive and to forget the hurts of the past so we can move on to a new life and a new season.

Joseph had a lot to forget. He refused to dwell on the past. He let go of the feelings of resentment, self-pity, and disappointment. The brain permanently keeps our memories, but we don't have to let everything in the past occupy our thoughts. We get to choose the things we dwell on. The Bible says, "Whatever is true, whatever is noble, whatever is right, whatever is pure, whatever is lovely, whatever is admirable—if anything is excellent or praiseworthy—think about such things" (Phil. 4:8).

Joseph learned to forget his dysfunctional family. His family was a blended one due to polygamy; twelve sons had been born to four different mothers, and that brought some intense sibling rivalry. His father favored Joseph, which in turn caused his brothers to be jealous of him. His father failed to support him when he reported his dream, so he felt rejected by his family. His brothers sold him as a slave. His family was as dysfunctional as they come.

Joseph also had to forget the disappointment of his lost young-adult years. He was in prison from the time he was about seventeen until he was about thirty. He missed out on those important years of his development, on the nurture of godly people in his life, and on the pursuit of his dreams. He was the object of abuse, rejection, and discrimination.

Joseph could have become another tragic case of a young person who had been given a great faith in God but then lost it because of the painful, disappointing circumstances of his life. He could have lost his faith the way a lot of people do, saying, "How could God let this happen to me?" But Joseph loved God and trusted Him. Joseph held on to the dream God had given him.

This has always been to me the most fascinating part of Joseph's story. Joseph held on to his faith and would not let anything or anyone take it away from him. When life got hard, he drew close to God. Many people turn away from God during times of intense trial and get angry with Him for allowing adversity to come into their lives, but not Joseph.

The same example Joseph showed us can be seen in the African American community today. African Americans endured the sin of slavery, yet the Christian faith is powerful among so many of them. We would think that people who had endured slavery would never have accepted the religion of their captors. Yet these people were able to transcend the sin of slave owners to receive the gospel of Jesus Christ. In the civil rights movement of the 1960s it was the gospel of Christ that was preached as the basis for equality among all people. Even in the darkness of slavery came the light of the gospel, and many people, as Joseph had done, rose above the suffering of their lives to hold on to their faith in God—a faith that eventually won the victory.

When we add it all up, Joseph had all the excuses he needed to cop out on life. He could have blamed God, his dysfunctional family, Potiphar's wife who had falsely accused him, twelve years in prison as an innocent man, or the person who had promised to help him when he was in prison but who later forget about him. But he chose to rise above it all and to live on a higher plane. Joseph's example confronts the victim mentality of our day that blames everyone and everything. You and I are not responsible for what happens to us, but we are responsible for how we deal with it. We can't choose our circumstances, but we can choose our attitude and our actions.

Joseph is a shining example to teach us that despite our family upbringing, cultural influences, poor role models, tragedies, and disappointments, God's grace can enable us to forget all our troubles and to move on to living a full life. God is able to heal our wounded hearts. He is able to cause us to forget—to release the pain, to forgive those who have hurt us, and to recapture our dreams.

What do you need God to help you forget? You've carried the memory long enough. The past has been an albatross around your neck long enough. God wants to bless you with Manasseh—to enable you to forget your trouble.

THE REST OF THE STORY

Joseph named his second son Ephraim, whose name tells us the rest of the story: "God has made me [twice] fruitful in the land of my suffering." There are two key phrases in this statement. First, God had made Joseph "twice fruitful."[5] Joseph had discovered that God gives *more* than enough for what we need. He wasn't just fruitful; he was twice fruitful. Egypt would survive seven years of a severe drought due to Joseph's exceptional administrative leadership. So the words *twice fruitful* are even more impressive when placed next to the word *famine*. God is able to make us twice fruitful, even in times of famine.

Then there is the phrase "in the land of my suffering." God's provision came after a long season of suffering. God doesn't always change our circumstances or take us out of the suffering we are going through, but He can and will make us fruitful in the season of suffering.

What have you lost? Whom have you lost? Do you spend your time thinking about all the painful things that have happened to you? It's time to turn your mind toward the future. God says to you, "Forget the former things; do not dwell on the past. See, I am doing a new thing!" (Isa. 43:18–19). Ask God to give you the blessings of forgetfulness and fruitfulness as you shake off the dust of hurt and get ready for a new season of God's provision in your life.

I want to share a letter I received from a young woman whose life so beautifully portrays this example:

> Dear Dr. Cooper,
> If anyone had told me even three years ago that God would: successfully call me to Him; heal me physically so I could return to work (I had been on disability for one year); heal the pain and anger of incest resulting in promiscuity; restore my innocence; forgive my abortion (after making its wrongness known to me); completely heal me of alcoholism and drug addiction (and smoking); restore my immediate family relationships, especially with the one who was my sexual abuser; and change my desires to match His regarding men, righteousness, and freedom, I probably would have laughed. In fact, I'd probably get angry at that person for wasting my time, because I thought a life of freedom was beyond me. Besides, why would God even bother with a sinner like me?
> Well, I want you to know that all these things listed and more have happened since I returned home

to Atlanta from San Francisco like the prodigal son. My parents opened their hearts and arms to me and, along with my sister, showed me the gospel of Jesus Christ that, as you've been teaching, is freedom. I'm not sure why He bothers with a sinner like me, only now I'm in absolute amazement and gratitude, not in fear of rejection. What a mighty and good God I have come to know…and now He uses me to bless others with His gospel of freedom. What a privilege. I only know a little bit, but I guess that's all it takes. As I go along, sometimes smooth sailing toward rough terrain, I thank God for His Son and for all those who continue to tell the truth about who He is.

Just as He did with Joseph, God made Stephanie forget the troubles of her past and made her twice fruitful in the land of her suffering. He will do the same for you and for me.

Chapter 4

IT'S NOT MY FAULT!

Getting Rid of Excuses

W HEN I WAS in college studying psychology, I read a
book that made a lifelong impression on me. William Glasser in *Reality Therapy* says that man is
not irresponsible because he is ill; he is ill because he is irresponsible.[1] That's another way of saying we make ourselves sick
by our poor choices and irresponsible actions. It also means we
can make ourselves well by making good decisions and taking
responsibility for our actions.

While so much of the dust that we need to shake off comes
from what others have done to us and from life situations, the
story would not be complete without talking about some of the
problems we create ourselves. At times we are our own worst
enemy. Irresponsibility is the root cause of many of our problems, not the symptom. We practice self-defeating behaviors,
and we need to become aware of those behaviors and take personal responsibility for changing them so that we will act in
ways that make us victorious. God designed us to reign in life,
not to be defeated in life.

If all we do is focus on what others have done to us or the
opportunities we've missed or the bad breaks we've gotten, we
will end up feeling sorry for ourselves. We have to see ourselves

as being in charge of our own destiny. We are God-created but self-molded. We have a direct role to play in our own development. The Holy Spirit shapes us, but we must be yielded and obedient to Him. That means we have to decide the kind of person we want to be and the kind of life we want to live—and go for it.

Victims feel weak. People who take responsibility feel powerful. We empower ourselves when we take responsibility for our lives. Power comes when we stop focusing on what has happened to us and start focusing on what we are going to make happen.

When we are disappointed, hurt, or angry, we tend to focus our thoughts and feelings on what others have done to us and the negative things that have happened to us. When we do that, we get stuck in that place emotionally. We talk to our friends and family about what happened, rehearsing the details over and over. We feel like victims, and we even feel sorry for ourselves. Instead of learning from our experiences, we waste them, often choosing instead to repeat unhealthy patterns. Even when difficult things happen to us, we can learn things about ourselves and make improvements in our own lives.

If we get fired from a job, experience a failed relationship, have a fight with our family, suffer financial problems, or go through business setbacks, but we can't see the part we played in those problems, we're not looking at the full picture. We tend to focus on the things that others have done wrong and fail to see how we are also responsible. Don't feel threatened at the thought of taking an honest look at yourself. That's really the key to a healthy life. As I mentioned earlier, Socrates said, "The unexamined life is not worth living."[2] The psalmist David prayed, "Search me, O God, and know my heart" (Ps. 139:23). Paul said, "Examine yourselves...test yourselves" (2 Cor. 13:5). We live in the "age of victimization." Victimization cries, "It's not my fault!" Victimization blames other people and circumstances for one's predicament; it blocks the pathway to personal responsibility and engages in endless self-pity. Today we have no-fault automobile insurance, no-fault divorces, and no-fault moral choices.

Your life is God's gift to you, and what you do with your life is your gift to God. "Each of us will give an account of himself to God" (Rom. 14:12). "Yes, but" is the confession of every failure. Winners, however, take responsibility and don't make excuses or blame others. Passing the buck is the great American pastime. We will never succeed until we take charge of our lives and stop making excuses and blaming others.

Social scientist Charles Sykes tells the story of an FBI agent who embezzled two thousand dollars and used it for gambling. When he was fired for his crime, the agent went to court and successfully argued that his behavior was a handicap, protected under the Americans with Disabilities Act. And the FBI was forced to reinstate him![3]

Making excuses is as old as time itself. It's our nature to make excuses. When Adam and Eve sinned, God came looking for them in the Garden of Eden. "What have you done?" God asked. Adam blamed Eve and God. Eve, in turned, blamed the devil (Gen. 3:8–13). God asks each of us, "What have you done?" He doesn't ask, "What have others done to you?" He doesn't ask, "What privileges have you been denied?" He doesn't ask, "Were you raised in a dysfunctional family?" He doesn't ask, "Did your parents neglect you?" He doesn't ask, "Has society treated you unfairly?" He asks, "What have you done?"

Consider this statement: "For since the creation of the world God's invisible qualities—his eternal power and divine nature—have been clearly seen, being understood from what has been made, so that men are without excuse" (Rom. 1:20). We have no excuse. When we come to the place at which we say to ourselves, "I have no excuse," we are on our way to success.

Excuses We All Make

Here are three common excuses we all use: "I didn't do it." "It wasn't so bad." "Yes, but..." Let's take a closer look at these three excuses.

"I didn't do it."

We make this excuse by denying what we did, telling lies, or blaming others. In the Old Testament there is a story about the people of Israel making an idol in the form of a golden calf. They did this when Moses was on the mountain receiving the Ten Commandments from God. They pressured Moses's older brother, Aaron, who was their priest, to make the calf. When Moses came down the mountain holding the stone tablets inscribed with the Ten Commandments, he saw the calf and the people dancing around it in worship. He was furious and threw down the tablets, breaking them into pieces. He then destroyed the golden calf.

Now get this. He asked his brother, Aaron, "What did these people do to you, that you led them into such great sin?" (Exod. 32:21). Then comes one of the biggest excuses in history. Aaron replied, "You know how prone these people are to evil" (v. 22). (Notice he immediately shifts the blame to the people instead of himself.) "They gave me the gold, and I threw it into the fire, and out came this calf!" (v. 24). Now that is unbelievable. Aaron couldn't tell a very good lie or even make a halfway believable excuse. He flat out said, "I didn't do it," when he had done it.

It seems today that our culture is incapable of saying the word *lie*. When the news media uncover some politician or public figure who has told a lie, they don't use the word *lie*; they say something like "He wasn't completely forthright" or "She wasn't totally honest." The fact is, these people weren't honest at all. It wasn't that they didn't tell the truth; it is that they lied. They intentionally said something they knew was false in order to mislead others and to avoid taking responsibility.

"It wasn't so bad."

This excuse downplays our bad behavior. We end up justifying ourselves instead of confronting what we did wrong and taking responsibility to make it right. Sometimes our minds won't face the truth, so we lie to ourselves. The lies we tell ourselves may be more destructive than the ones we tell others. We have to learn to be honest with ourselves and to face up to the facts instead of making light of things that are serious. The Bible tells us, "Through the commandment [of God] sin might become utterly sinful" (Rom. 7:13). That means that instead of minimizing our sins, we should face them as sin—not calling them mistakes, errors in judgment, or bad habits. We need the Word of God so that "sin might be recognized as sin" (v. 13). Once we recognize our actions for what they are, we can confess our sins to God and know that we are forgiven!

Fulton Sheen spoke at the National Prayer Breakfast during Jimmy Carter's presidency. He began his address, "Mr. President, Mrs. Carter, my fellow sinners..." Once he had everyone's attention, he went on to talk about sin and God's cure for sin.[4]

When we go to the doctor, the first thing he or she does is

perform an examination and run tests to find out what's wrong. Then the doctor makes a prognosis and gives a prescription for healing. We can't have a plan for recovery until we first have a diagnosis.

When the doctor says, "You have the flu," we don't get angry and say, "No, I don't." We face the fact that we have the flu. Then we follow the directions for healing. The same is true with our thoughts, feelings, and actions. We have to face the facts about how we think, how we treat others, how we communicate, and so forth in order to make the changes needed for us to live healthy lives. As long as we are in denial and we lie to ourselves, we will stay the way we are. Once we accept the facts about ourselves, we are on the road to recovery and change.

"Yes, but…"

This excuse begins well but finishes poorly. We admit we were wrong, but then we undo it with an excuse. We let ourselves off the hook instead of taking responsibility. We say things like "I couldn't help it," "I didn't mean to," or "It wasn't really me." We blame our behavior on our mood, our personality, or our temper. There is certainly nothing wrong with explaining our actions, but explaining ourselves and making excuses are different things. Excuses are a dead-end street. As long as we live by excuses, we stay just the way we are and fail to grow into the people God created us to be. Shake off the dust of excuses, follow God's plan for healing, and watch your life and relationships begin to flourish.

What's Wrong With Excuses?

Making excuses weakens our character. It's like what happens when we lie. After telling one lie, it's easier to tell another. We begin to believe our excuses. Whatever we tell ourselves long enough, we start believing, and what we believe, we become. Proverbs says, "As he thinks within himself, so he is" (Prov. 23:7, NAS).

Our character is the most valuable asset we have. Our character consists of our beliefs, values, and ethics. Character is like a compass that guides us true north and keeps us on track. When our character is faulty and weak, we lose our way spiritually and morally. When we make excuses, we lie to ourselves and become spiritually weaker. When we speak the truth, we become strong on the inside, and that inner strength of character enables us to handle the pressures and problems of life with victory.

Making excuses keeps us from reaching our goals. We need goals to get ahead in life. Without goals we drift. Goals give us direction. They give us markers by which to measure ourselves. When we make excuses rather than making goals, we let ourselves off the hook instead of challenging ourselves to do better. Now we all fail to reach our goals at times; we all come up short. But when we do, let's look inside ourselves and take stock as to what the real issues are and then address those issues head-on without making excuses.

Excuses keep us from learning valuable lessons from our experiences. We take the focus off ourselves and put it on others or on circumstances. We blame our family, the people at work, the economy, politicians, and even genetics. We blame anyone and anything to lead us to the conclusion, "It's not my fault." And the whole time we receive a failing grade in the school of life and end up repeating the same mistakes because we don't take responsibility for ourselves.

Am I saying that we are to blame for everything that happens to us? Absolutely not! We all experience hard times, injustices, and circumstances that are beyond our control. But I am saying that we should not focus on those things. We should focus on what we can do in the face of those experiences so that we can take charge of our destiny and avoid feeling as if we're victims of what has happened to us. We should focus our thoughts and conversations on what we can learn and do to move on with our lives.

Sitting in a coffee shop, I overheard a group of people talking at a table nearby. One angry young woman told the others about how someone had hurt and offended her. She asked them, "What could ever happen that would make me forgive her?" I wanted to say, "The cross of Christ happened. He died for your sins and for mine so that we may be forgiven. Since He forgives us, we can forgive others."

OK, I'm Ready to Shake My Excuses

The first words recorded in the Bible that God spoke to Adam after He created him began with the phrase "You are free..." (Gen. 2:16). God told Adam he was free to eat of any tree in the garden except one. Most people have heard about that one forbidden tree. But I want to focus on just those first three words: "You are free..." Think of the power of that statement. What if we realized today that we are free—totally free to make any decision we want to make. We are free to go any direction we want to go. God has a plan and purpose for our lives, a destiny for which we were created, but He gave us the freedom to choose whether we would follow His plan or chase after our own. Our destiny lies in our decisions.

Our choices today will determine our destiny tomorrow. God is the source of our hope for a bright future. The good news is that we have options. We're not trapped in our circumstances. We can change. Life can change—because we are free to choose!

Let the power of God's words sink in deeply. When you feel depressed, trapped, or hopeless, tell yourself, "I am free. I don't have to stay where I am. I don't have to keep doing what I am doing. I don't have to put up with this situation. I am free!" Those three words will cause us to begin to see opportunities and options that we never saw before. When we accept the fact that we are free, we will start dreaming instead of despairing about our lives.

Freedom, however, requires responsibility. Once we exercise our freedom to make certain choices, we are responsible for those decisions. Responsibility means taking charge of your life. Stop blaming others, whining about circumstances, or complaining about situations. Decide to make the changes you want to make.

Responsibility also equals empowerment. When we take responsibility for our own lives, we gain a new sense of self-respect. We feel good about ourselves and our accomplishments. Self-esteem is based on self-respect, which comes from what we achieve and from who we are outside of our accomplishments. Positive self-esteem is a fringe benefit of responsible living!

Many people live as though their actions do not affect anyone else—but they do. When we make an important decision, it is like throwing a pebble in a pond, which creates an ever-widening circle of waves that affect the people around us, either positively or negatively. Taking responsibility for our actions means considering how what we do affects others.

Freedom plus responsibility equals accountability—accountability to God and to others for how we exercise our freedom to choose. "So then, each of us will give an account of himself to God" (Rom. 14:12). Jesus said, "From everyone who has been given much, much will be demanded" (Luke 12:48). Thinking and acting like a victim is a dead-end street for anyone who wants to live a full life.

We have to assume responsibility for our lives and be accountable to God if we want to live a blessed life. Even Moses told the people of his day, "All these blessings will come upon you and accompany you *if you obey the Lord your God*" (Deut. 28:2, emphasis added). Notice the connection between obedience, or accountability, and blessings.

Viktor Frankl, a Jewish physician who survived Hitler's death camps, said, "Everything can be taken from a man but one thing: the last of the human freedoms—to choose one's attitude in any given set of circumstances, to choose one's own way."[5] He found meaning in life even in the Nazi camps and was able to survive and to help others do the same.

Max Lucado says, "If there are a thousand steps between us and him, he will take all but one. But he will leave the final one for us. The choice is ours."[6] God does not force us to love and obey Him. The choice is ours.

When we learn to exercise our God-given freedom with responsibility and accountability, we will be victors instead of victims. No one can succeed with a victim mentality. To be sure, there are real victims of crime, discrimination, and injustice. But I am talking about the attitude in which a person refuses to take personal responsibility. The victim cries, "It's not my fault." The victim demands, "The world owes me a living!" What happens to us is not our fault, but what we do in response to what happens to us is our responsibility. You and I make the choice: victim or victor?

+ The victim says, "I can't." The victor says, "I can do everything through him who gives me strength" (Phil. 4:13).

+ The victim says, "It's not my fault!" The victor says, "I am responsible for my actions."

+ The victim says, "We never did it that way before." The victor says, "Nothing ventured, nothing gained."

+ The victim lives in fear. The victor walks by faith.

+ The victim sees problems. The victor sees opportunities.

+ The victim strikes back. The victor turns the other cheek.

+ The victim harbors resentment. The victor forgives as God forgives.

+ The victim gives up. The victor presses on.

+ The victim explains why it can't be done. The victor believes it can be done.

+ The victim offers excuses. The victor sets an example.

+ The victim says, "With man this is impossible." The victor says, "With God all things are possible!"

+ The victim says, "The odds are against us." The victor says, "If God is for us, who can be against us?" (Rom. 8:31).

I've always been inspired by the life of Booker T. Washington. Washington grew up in the days of the worst racial discrimination. As a child he was deprived of an education, although he wanted to study. Yet when he was a young man, he fulfilled his dream of a formal education and then became an influential leader in our nation. He said, "I have learned that success is to be measured not so much by the position that one has reached in life as by the obstacles which he has overcome while trying to succeed."[7] Instead of being a victim of discrimination, he was a victor.

There's a thought-provoking line in the book *Gone With the Wind*: "There ain't nothin' from the outside can lick any of us."[8] It's what is on the inside that defeats us—attitudes of fear, pessimism, resentment, and negativism.

Helen Keller was a victor. Although blind and deaf, she refused to play the role of a victim. She shows us how to rise above victimization in her poem "They Took Away":

> They took away what should have been my eyes,
> (But I remembered Milton's Paradise).
> They took away what should have been my ears,
> (Beethoven came and wiped away my tears).
> They took away what should have been my tongue,
> (But I had talked with God when I was young).
> He would not let them take away my soul—
> Possessing that, I still possess the whole.[9]

Before we leave this thought of being a victor, let me share an incredible story of a high school graduate of the class of 1996 named Camara Barrett. Camara was valedictorian when he graduated from Thomas Jefferson High School in Brooklyn,

New York. He was also class president, editor of the school paper, a peer tutor, and an award-winning public speaker.

So it's no surprise that Camara was accepted by eight universities and went on to Cornell University on a scholarship. The surprise is that he achieved all this while living in a homeless shelter. After a bitter conflict with his parents when he was a teenager, he had found himself out on the street. For several days he lived and studied on the subway at night, getting off to go to school during the day.

After the people at Thomas Jefferson High helped Camara get settled in a homeless shelter, he pulled his grades back up, studied diligently for his SATs, and applied for college.[10] Rather than destroying him, the experience of being alone strengthened his resolve to study and to do something with his life. He was a victor instead of a victim. You can be too!

Chapter 5

MY LIFE IN RUINS

Coming Back From Ruin

THE MOVIE TITLE *My Life in Ruins* aptly describes the way we all feel at times. We feel like we've made a mess of things or that other people close to us have ruined everything. A ruined business. A ruined marriage. Ruined finances.

That's how the people of Israel felt after the Babylonian army destroyed Jerusalem. The Babylonians had leveled the magnificent temple of King Solomon to the ground, and the people were taken into captivity to serve in Babylon (Jer. 52:1–27). The prophet Jeremiah had cautioned the king of Judah not to provoke the king of Babylon and to return to serving God, but neither the king nor the people listened to the counsel of Jeremiah (Jer. 22:1–5; 27:12–15).

After the war and the exile Jeremiah wrote his Lamentations over the fall of the city. Everything was in ruins. What is worse is that God had allowed it to happen. That's what troubles us all. The Israelites were God's covenant people, and Jerusalem was even called the city of God (Dan. 9:16). But now the city was destroyed, and the people were in captivity.

The Israelites were right back where they had started. Their story had begun with their deliverance from Egypt, where they had been slaves for four hundred years, and now they were in exile in Babylon.

God had placed a calling on the Israelites' lives and given them a purpose to fulfill, but now everything was ruined. They were far from home in Babylon, and they were just as far from God's purpose for their lives. You see, even though we are God's people and God has a purpose for our lives, He allows us to make our own decisions. The Israelites made the wrong decisions, and they suffered the consequences as a result. We can't blame God for the consequences of our decisions. The Israelites were in captivity because of their own choices, not because of God.

What's more is that sometimes everything is ruined not because of our choices but because of the choices of other people in our lives. Sometimes we are victims of what others have done. Since we are connected to others by our relationships, what one person does affects everyone around that person. One person can disrupt an entire family. A few greedy business people can bring a corporation down. A corrupt politician can wreak havoc through failed political policies. Many of the people who were taken captive by the Babylonians hadn't done anything wrong. They had worshipped God while others had served idols. They had listened to the word of God that Jeremiah had preached, while the leaders had rejected the prophet's message.

Our actions and decisions affect those around us in the same way a pebble thrown into a pond affects the water around it with ever-widening circles. We need to think about the consequences of our important decisions not only for how they will affect us but also how they will impact others. We need to hold ourselves accountable for our decisions, knowing that we have an obligation to make decisions that honor God, benefit others, and bring us good, not harm. Careless decisions can affect a lot of people for a long time. And that's the story of the Israelites in the Babylonian captivity.

I'm sure the Israelites felt that God had given up on them. It's easy to think, as perhaps the Israelites did, that the reason we are facing ruin is because of some mysterious plan of God to test us. But God is not out to ruin us. We experience ruin because of our choices or the choices of others that affect us. Jesus said, "In this world you will have trouble" (John 16:33). He didn't say, "You will have trouble from God." Life brings us trouble because we live in a sinful, imperfect world.

What we tell ourselves and how we make sense out of suffering, ruin, and difficulty will determine whether we become casualties of our circumstances or conquerors. The quality of our lives will never be higher than the level of our thinking. If we tell ourselves that God is against us, that He is bringing trouble on us, then we will lose our faith and go into the depths of despair. If we tell ourselves that everything is ruined and can never be restored, then we will give up hope and accept defeat. But we can tell ourselves the truth even when life is bad: God is faithful even though people are faithless, and what is impossible with human power is possible with God.

That's what Jeremiah did. He changed his way of thinking, and when he did, he became hopeful. As he penned the words of his laments over the fall of the city of Jerusalem, he vented his fears, frustrations, and depression. He wrote what is now considered the most depressing book in the Bible: Lamentations. If we were to title that book today, we would call it The Blues. A lament is a poem or song that expresses our deepest feelings of sadness and despair. Read the depths of Jeremiah's despair:

How deserted lies the city,
  once so full of people!
How like a widow is she,
  who once was great among the nations!
She who was queen among the provinces
  has now become a slave....
"Look, O Lord, and consider,
  for I am despised."...

"This is why I weep
  and my eyes overflow with tears.
No one is near to comfort me,
  no one to restore my spirit....
The Lord is righteous,
  yet I rebelled against his command....
See, O Lord, how distressed I am!
  I am in torment within,
and in my heart I am disturbed,
  for I have been most rebellious...."

I have been deprived of peace;
  I have forgotten what prosperity is.
So I say, "My splendor is gone
  and all that I had hoped for from the Lord."
...my soul is downcast within me.
  —Lamentations 1:1–20; 3:17–20

I told you it's a depressing book. And that's just a small portion of the lament that he wrote; he poured out page after page in Lamentations. But suddenly, almost out of nowhere, Jeremiah slammed on the brakes and turned his mind toward another theme. As soon as he changed his thinking, his emotions started to change, and he began to write powerful words of hope. Look at what he wrote: "Yet this I call to mind and there-fore I have hope" (Lam. 3:21).

Now that is a powerful statement worth our consideration. The word *yet* means that despite everything that had happened, the prophet had hope. Jeremiah's outlook on life turned on the hinge of this phrase: "This I call to mind." To call something to mind means to intentionally think about that thing. It's what we call to mind that determines the quality of our lives. If we call to mind our failure, we will lose our confidence. If we call to mind the irresponsibility of others, we will be angry. If we call to mind the limitations of our circumstances, we will forfeit our faith. But if we call to mind the promises of God, we will have hope.

You see, it's how we think about what's happened to us and how we make sense out of suffering that determines how well we deal with it. So what did Jeremiah call to mind that cat-apulted him out of the depths of depression to the heights of hope? Here is what he started to think about:

> Because of the LORD's great love, we are not
>   consumed,
>   for his compassions never fail.
> They are new every morning;
>   great is your faithfulness.
> I say to myself, "The LORD is my portion;
>   therefore I will wait for him."
> —LAMENTATIONS 3:22–24

We have to wade through three chapters of laments before we find that jewel in Lamentations. What amazing words of hope. We too can spend weeks, months, or even years in the depths of despair thinking that everything is ruined and will never be restored, and then in one moment turn our thoughts toward the faithfulness of God and rise above our disappointments on the wings of hope. Let's look closer at Jeremiah's words and think about these powerful truths.

"Because of the Lord's great love, we are not consumed."

Even though we've been attacked, destroyed, and taken into captivity, we're still here! We're still standing. We are not consumed. Since we are still here and we're still standing, we can make a comeback! Why? Because of the Lord's great love. God's love is great. His love is eternal. Nothing "will be able to separate us from the love of God" (Rom. 8:39). Because of the Lord's great love we can be forgiven, we can be restored, and we can overcome every problem we face.

"His compassions never fail."

The word *compassions* could also be translated "mercies." (See, for example, Lamentations 3:22, NLT). Compassion is the action of passion. I think of passion as a feeling and of compassion as an action. When we are moved with passion, we respond with compassion toward others. Love is what God feels for us; compassion is that attitude God extends toward us. God is merciful. People are judgmental, but God is merciful. God will give us a second chance when people give up on us. It is true that God allowed the Israelites to go through a horrible season of suffering. But the difficulty was the result of their choices, not because of what God did. God's compassions and mercies did not fail them. Their story is one of human failure, not of God's failure.

What is mercy? In order to understand mercy, we also need to understand grace, as they are two sides of a coin. *Grace* is a word with which we are familiar because of the song "Amazing

Grace," written some four hundred years ago by John Newton. Grace is the extension of a free gift. Grace is God giving us forgiveness, salvation, and blessing even though we don't deserve it. We don't work for salvation. It is the gift of God.

Mercy is expressed in the opposite way. While grace is God giving us what we don't deserve, mercy is God *not* giving us what we *do* deserve. God withholds the judgment that we deserve for our sin because of what Jesus did for us on the cross. God is long-suffering and patient with us, not wanting anyone to perish but for everyone to experience His saving grace.

What is more, Jeremiah discovered that God's mercies are new every morning. The morning brings a sense of hope. The rising of the sun dispels the darkness of the night and puts us in a good mood. Every morning life starts over for us. We have a new day to live. The morning sweeps away the disappointments of yesterday. Jeremiah discovered that every new day brings new mercies from God that can overcome the failures of the past. Yesterday may have been in ruins, but today is a new day of restoration because of the mercy of God.

I was driving to my office one morning, thinking about the mercy of God. Suddenly I began to sing these words that flowed from my heart:

> Lord, I love You. I bow before You.
> You are worthy of my praise.
> You are holy, clothed in splendor.
> I will sing through endless days.
> For Your mercies, never ceasing.
> They are new every morn.
> Your compassions never failing
> Keep me safe throughout the storm.
> Hallelujah to the Father.

Hallelujah to the Son.
Hallelujah to the Spirit,
For Your love, bright as the sun.[1]

I kept singing the song until I got to my office, and I recorded it so I wouldn't forget it. I have performed it hundreds of times in services, concerts, prisons, and even homeless shelters to help people call to mind the mercies of God so that they will have hope. Since God's mercies are new every morning, then whatever has been ruined can be restored. Yesterday was a day of ruin, but today is a day of restoration.

"Great is your faithfulness."

This statement from Lamentations 3:23 is referenced in the majestic song "Great Is Thy Faithfulness." Faithfulness is dependability and reliability. Healthy relationships are based on faithfulness. Few things in life are more disappointing than people who break their promises or violate our trust. The Israelites in exile needed to know that God would still be faithful to His promises and that they could count on Him to restore them to their former glory if they would turn their hearts toward Him.

So Jeremiah says, "I will wait for him" (v. 24). God's love is eternal, His mercy is infinite, and His faithfulness is great. We can trust Him and wait for His perfect timing and His great power to restore what has been ruined. When we call to mind the mercy and faithfulness of God, we can move from the theme of "my life in ruins" to "my life in restoration." When we have hope, we will stop telling all our friends and family about the ruin we have experienced and start thinking instead about the restoration God is bringing. When we stop praying about the ruin, we will start praising God for the restoration.

Turn your thoughts away from the ruin you have experienced, and turn your thoughts toward the restoration that God has in store for you. Stop looking back at what has happened and look forward to what *can* happen!

When Jeremiah became hopeful, he wanted to give hope to others. So he sat down and wrote a letter to the exiles in Babylon that the leaders read to all the people (Jer. 29:1–23). This is an amazing letter filled with the promises of God and with the steps necessary for the Israelites to turn their ruin into restoration. Jeremiah told the exiles first that they would be in Babylon only for seventy years. So they needed to mentally prepare themselves for their return home.

It is important that we have a vision for where we are going so that we don't get comfortable where we are. God promises a time limit on our suffering. "Weeping may remain for a night, but rejoicing comes in the morning" (Ps. 30:5).

Even though one generation of the Israelites would live their lives in Babylon, they would be able to tell their kids and grandkids, "Don't get used to living here. This is only temporary. You are not going to serve the king of Babylon. You are going home. God is going to deliver us. God is going to make a way out of here, even though we don't know exactly when He will do it. God has promised to deliver us. Your future is as bright as the promises of God are!"

That's what we have to tell ourselves, our families, and our friends when we are going through a time of ruin. "I'm not staying where I am. Things are not going to stay in ruins. I'm going to leave this season of difficulty. By the grace of God, I'm going back home. I'm going to rebuild what has been destroyed. I'm going to restore what has been ruined." Let me encourage you to stop seeing your life in ruins and to start seeing your life in restoration.

Jeremiah gave the exiles this promise from God: "'For I know the plans I have for you,' declares the LORD, 'plans to prosper you and not to harm you, plans to give you hope and a future'" (Jer. 29:11). That is God's promise to us. God is no respecter of persons. If God turned the ruin into restoration for His people then, He will do the same now for us.

God has plans for us and for our restoration, no matter what has been ruined in us and no matter why things are in a state of ruin. God went on to say to the Israelites through Jeremiah, "'Then you will call upon me and come and pray to me, and I will listen to you. You will seek me and find me when you seek me with all your heart. I will be found by you,' declares the LORD, 'and will bring you back from captivity'" (vv. 12–14). What a promise from God!

Do you need God to bring you back from captivity? Are you captive to failure? Captive to sin? Captive to divorce? Captive to guilt? Captive to bankruptcy? Captive to disappointment? Captive to fear? Have you been taken away from a life that was filled with joy, provision, and peace and now find yourself in spiritual and emotional exile? Has everything been ruined in your life and destroyed by either your poor choices or the poor choices of others? God tells us to come to Him and to pray to Him, and He says that He will listen to us. Seek Him today with all your heart, and He will bring you back from captivity and restore everything in your life that has been ruined.

Chapter 6

THERE'S NOTHING TO
FEAR BUT FEAR ITSELF

Facing Down Fear

I N 1929 THE stock market on Wall Street crashed. For-
tunes were lost overnight. People made a run on the banks
and were unable to withdraw their money. Panic gripped
America. The nation was plunged into the Great Depression.

The Great Depression left its mark on the American people.
Economists keep the event alive in our minds, even though most
of us were not even born when it occurred. The Great Depression
injected fear into the American psyche. It's always looming out
there, ready to happen again when we least expect it.

During his 1933 inaugural address President Franklin
Roosevelt sought to calm a troubled America in the throes of
depression by saying, "The only thing we have to fear is fear
itself."[1] President Roosevelt understood that there were two
challenges facing the nation: the crisis without and the fear
within. The fear within us is always a greater crisis than the
problems around us. Fear is the enemy that defeats our dreams,
our hopes, and our plans. Fear spreads like a disease, and
President Roosevelt understood that fact. Once we start sharing
our fears and giving voice to our fears, other people become

afraid as well. Robert Louis Stevenson said, "Keep your fears to yourself, but share your courage with others."[2]

Everyone battles fear. Don't ever let people tell you they aren't afraid or that they never worry. They do. We all do. Learning to face our fears and to share our fears with others is the first step in overcoming them. Fear won't go away by itself. Fear won't get tired of fighting our hopes and dreams. Fear will keep fighting us. We have to face our fears—know what they are, put a name to them, understand where they come from—and then fight our fears with faith. We are the only ones who can free ourselves from our fears.

Fear is a feeling of dread, alarm, panic, and anxiety. Fear is not a sin. We don't need to confuse morality and emotion. Fear is a natural emotion that gives us a sense of caution and of boundaries that protect us. But our fears often become unhealthy. Fear ranges from mild anxiety to crippling panic attacks to chronic phobias. Louis Pasteur, father of "germ theory" and "bacteriology," had an obsessive fear of dirt and infection. It is said that he often refused to shake hands, meticulously cleaned his plates and utensils before eating, and astonished dinner guests by taking out a portable microscope to ensure plates were clean.[3] President and Mrs. Benjamin Harrison were so afraid of the new electricity installed in the White House that they didn't turn the lights on for weeks.[4]

Here are the top ten global fears:

1. Fear of public speaking (glossophobia)

2. Fear of death (necrophobia)

3. Fear of spiders (arachnophobia)

4. Fear of darkness (scotophobia)

5. Fear of heights (acrophobia)

6. Fear of people or social situations (sociophobia)

7. Fear of flying (aerophobia)

8. Fear of open spaces (agoraphobia)

9. Fear of thunder and lightning (brontophobia)

10. Fear of confined spaces (claustrophobia)[5]

The American Psychiatric Association has categorized a variety of phobias. A phobia is an intense, extreme fear that keeps a person from functioning. I have claustrophobia, and I know where it came from. When I was a small boy, my older brother Bill and his friend talked me into seeing if I could fit on the shelf of the cedar closet in the hallway of our house. Naively I crawled in between the shelves. Then Bill and his friend slammed the door and held it closed while I went nuts! Finally, after enough of my screaming, they opened the door. I fell out on the floor, terrified, while they had a good laugh. When I smell the scent of cedar wood to this day, I think of the closed-in space of that closet.

A common fear today is agoraphobia. This word was taken from the Greek word *agora*, meaning "the market place."[6] The agora was the public square downtown where people did all their shopping. Fear of the marketplace, or fear of being in public, keeps some people locked inside their home as recluses. They are terrified that something bad may happen to them if they come outside. The fact is, it will! But taking the risks of life is better than missing out on life altogether.

I have a friend who told me that she is afraid of elevators. She takes the stairs everywhere she goes. She never gets in an elevator. I worked with her in a few counseling sessions to try to help her understand her fear and to defeat it. Then the day came when I got her into an elevator to see if she could handle it. She made it through that grueling experience, but I thought she was going to have a nervous breakdown. After that elevator ride my friend told me that she would rather live with her fear and take the steps. She hasn't been on an elevator since.

Where does fear come from? Research indicates that we are born with only two fears: the fear of falling and the fear of loud noises. All other fears are learned responses. Think about that fact. Fear is a way of thinking. We learn to be afraid through early childhood experiences, and then we generalize those fears to other situations when we become adults. All adult fears are childhood fears in a new grown-up form. We do outgrow some of our childhood fears, like fear of the dark. I had a fear of clowns as a kid, but I don't have it today (which is a good thing for a grown man).

I have a fear of snakes, as I'm sure many of you do. I developed it after watching an episode of *The Rifleman*, which was one of my favorite television shows when I was a boy. In this particular episode the rifleman, Lucas McCain, and his son were traveling. They met Micah, their sheriff friend who was transporting a prisoner, and they all slept out under the stars as people always do in westerns. When McCain woke up in the morning, there was a rattlesnake coiled up by his leg, under his blanket. The entire half-hour show involved McCain lying completely still, sweating profusely, while his son and the sheriff tried to figure out a way to get the rattlesnake out. The prisoner kept offering to help, since he saw it as a good opportunity to escape, so finally the sheriff allowed it.

The snake never moved except to shake his rattle with great

intensity as though he was furious over the whole ordeal. Finally, in the last sixty seconds of the program, McCain had endured all he could (and the show was about over), so the prisoner grabbed the snake in McCain's blanket and threw it at the sheriff. Then he grabbed a gun and started to turn. The sheriff quickly fired at the prisoner, killing him, then pumped several shots into the rattlesnake.[7] That was the whole show—thirty minutes of terror conditioning fear into everybody watching. It was a thriller disguised as a western.

After watching that show, I can't tell you how often as a boy I got up at night and looked under the bed to see if there was a snake there. Or worse, I would kick the covers back because in my mind I could feel that rattlesnake lying by my feet. I still think about that show to this day and can feel the fear it created in me. It's the only episode of *The Rifleman* I can remember, and I watched every one of them.

I am terrified of snakes to this day. I wouldn't even visit the reptile house when Barbie and I used to take our kids to the zoo. I would make the excuse that I was going to get some sodas and popcorn while Barbie and the kids went to see the snakes. You see, our fears are learned through experiences and often take different forms as we become adults. Now here's an important truth: since fear is learned, it has to be unlearned. The key to conquering fear is to change the way we think and the things we believe about whatever we are afraid of.

Fear comes in many shapes and sizes. The fear of failure, for example, keeps people from trying something new or taking a risk. If we want to succeed in life, we'd better get used to failure. Winston Churchill said, "Success consists of going from failure to failure without loss of enthusiasm."[8]

The fear of success is another one. This sets in *after* we gain success. Many successful people live with the constant fear that something bad is going to happen and will take all their success away. Jesus told a story about a wealthy business owner who gave three of his managers large sums of money and told them to invest the funds for a return. The first two made investments and got good returns, but the third man took his money and buried it in the ground. When the owner called for a financial account of what each man had done, he commended the first two but reprimanded the third man for not producing anything. When asked why he had hidden the money instead of investing it, the third man simply said, "I was afraid." (See Matthew 25:14–30.) When you are in a season of success, enjoy it, and continue to make investments for greater success.

The fear of rejection and hurt keeps people from forming close relationships. People who have this fear maintain their distance from others. Cynically they tell themselves such false ideas as "You can't trust anyone," "People always let you down," and "Don't get too close or you'll get hurt." Fear may insulate us from hurt, but it will also isolate us from love. It's better to love and to get hurt than not to love at all. Not to love is not really to live.

The fear of disease is called hypochondriasis. One man I know lived in constant fear of getting sick, and he worried his family with his thinking that he was going to catch this sickness or that one every time he heard about a new disease or virus going around. The fact is, he rarely got sick, and he finally died in his nineties of natural causes. But he had these words inscribed on his grave marker: "See, I told you I was sick!"

When we go to the doctor and fill out a medical history of our family, it makes us start thinking about the illnesses our parents or grandparents had and which ones we might contract.

I have a friend in his late thirties who told me about his father dying of a heart attack when he was only fifty-four. As I listened to my friend's concerns, I said, "You're not going to die of heart failure like your dad did. You're going to die of worry if you don't stop thinking about it."

The information age has made us fear the future like never before. We aren't aware only of the problems facing America. The constant barrage of global news makes us aware of every problem in the world. Since news agencies focus mostly on bad news, it makes it even worse, as awareness creates anxiety about global world conditions. Jesus prophesied that in the last days people "will faint from terror, apprehensive of what is coming on the world" (Luke 21:26).

The greatest fear is the fear of death. What lies beyond the grave? The age-old question of the biblical character Job still concerns us: "If a man dies, will he live again?" (Job 14:14). Jesus Christ called His message of the kingdom of God "good news." His first message was, "The kingdom of God is near. Repent and believe the good news!" (Mark 1:15). What is the good news that He announced? It is that if we receive Jesus as our Savior, we don't have to fear death. Jesus defeated sin and death by His resurrection, and He gives us eternal life.

I once read that there are 7,847 promises of God to His people in the Bible. Now, I don't know who counted all those promises, but one thing is for sure—God has a promise for every problem we face. Consider this: "Since the children have flesh and blood, he [Jesus] too shared in their humanity so that by his death he might destroy him who holds the power of death—that is, the devil—and free those who all their lives were held in slavery by their fear of death" (Heb. 2:14–15). What a graphic description of fear is found in the phrase "held in slavery by their fear." Fear is bondage, but faith brings freedom from fear.

Fear produces devastating effects. Fear paralyzes decision making, immobilizes action, hinders prayer, limits faith, restricts relationships, lowers productivity, jeopardizes health, and stifles joy.

FALSE EXPECTATIONS APPEARING REAL

The best definition of fear I've seen is an acronym from the word itself: False Expectations Appearing Real. The first step to defeating your fear is to analyze your fear and ask, "Is it real or imaginary?" A study from the University of Michigan showed the following:

+ Sixty percent of our fears will never happen.

+ Twenty percent are focused on our past, which is beyond our control.

+ Ten percent are so petty that they make no difference in our lives.

+ Of the remaining 10 percent, only 4 to 5 percent are real.[9]

The fact is that most of the things we are afraid of will never happen. We have to keep telling ourselves that fact so our fears do not take over our lives.

Late one night a little girl was awakened by a loud burst of thunder. She jumped out of bed and ran to her parents' room. "I want to get in bed with you and Dad," she told her mother.

"Sweetheart, there's nothing to be afraid of," replied her mother. "It's just a thunderstorm. Go back to bed. Nothing will harm you. You're too old to sleep in bed with us. Remember, God is in your room with you. He'll take care of you."

Ignoring her words, the little girl crawled into bed and got under the covers next to her father. She told her mother, "You go in there and sleep with God. I'm sleeping in here with Daddy!" Her expectations were obviously false, but they appeared real—and this little girl wasn't buying her mother's advice!

There is a legend about a traveler who while on his way to a village stopped his carriage to pick up an aged woman on the side of the road. The woman was dressed in a long black coat with her head and face covered. As they were traveling, the man was terrified when he realized that his guest was the dreaded plague cholera. The woman assured him that she would kill only ten people in the village. She even offered the traveler a strange-looking dagger and said, "If more than ten people die from the plague, you can kill me and end the plague." Arriving in the village, they discovered that more than a hundred people were already dead from the disease. The angry traveler lifted the dagger to destroy the plague, but she protested, "Wait! I killed only ten. Fear killed the rest."

When my son was about three years old, he developed a phobia of the vacuum cleaner. (Maybe that fear will come in handy for him when he gets married.) Every time the vacuum was turned on, he would get hysterical, run out of the room, and hide. He just knew the machine was going to suck him up. One Saturday morning my wife headed out to go to the grocery store. "Please vacuum while I'm gone," she asked. I assured her that I would. She left, and I proceeded to vacuum the family room, where my son happened to be watching cartoons. That was a mistake. As soon as I flipped the switch, my son went berserk and hid behind a chair. As he screamed uncontrollably, I thought to myself, "How can I get this kid over his fear?"

Suddenly it dawned on me that my son had a great love for the lawnmower. He loved to put his hands on the handle of the push mower and help me cut the grass.

"David Paul!" I called over his screaming little voice. "This isn't a vacuum cleaner; it's a lawnmower!" Almost immediately he grew calm and looked at me with a puzzled look. "It's a lawnmower," I said enthusiastically. "Come over here and help Dad mow the carpet." His face lit up with excitement, and he ran across the room and put his tiny hands on the handle of the vacuum cleaner. Off we went, mowing the carpet. We never again vacuumed the carpet; we mowed it. We had an outdoor lawnmower and an indoor lawnmower.

My son was suffering from a false expectation appearing real. That's all fear is. As long as my little boy expected the vacuum cleaner to suck him up, he panicked when it was turned on. We too have false beliefs. There are childish false beliefs, and there are adult false beliefs. The results are the same: fear, anxiety, and panic. As soon as my son changed his mind and decided the machine was a lawnmower and not a vacuum cleaner, his fear went away. His fear, as well as ours, was symptoms of what we believe. As soon as we change our minds about our false beliefs and start believing the truth, our fear will go away.

Perfect Love Drives Out Fear

Paul the apostle had a son in the faith whose name was Timothy. Timothy too battled fears and insecurities. Paul's final letter—which he wrote in prison shortly before Emperor Nero executed him in the city of Rome—was written to Timothy to help the younger man overcome his fears. Paul made a statement to

Timothy that shows some powerful truths about God and His relationship to us: "For God did not give us a spirit of timidity, but a spirit of power, of love and of self-discipline" (2 Tim. 1:7).

Timothy was a person of faith in God, but he was also fearful. Sounds like a contradiction, right? He was a man of faith and a man of fear. We all battle those polar forces within us. You see, faith is not the antidote to fear. This is a misconception many people have today. That's why we can have both fear and faith. How can we believe in God and His promises and yet have so much fear? It's because faith alone cannot conquer fear.

The opposite of fear is not faith; it's *love*. That's why the Bible says, "Perfect love drives out fear" (1 John 4:18). Perfect *faith* doesn't drive out fear; perfect *love* drives fear out of minds and hearts. We become afraid because we feel unloved and insecure in the world. Once we believe and know that God loves us and that He will be with us through everything in life, we overcome our fears.

There are only two primary emotions: love and fear. All other emotions come from these two. The Book of Genesis tells us that fear began with the sin of Adam and Eve. When these two sinned, they were afraid, and they hid from God in the Garden of Eden (Gen. 3:8). We've been hiding ever since, because we are afraid of God and afraid of each other. So we hide our true selves and believe that no one really loves us for who we are. We play games and try to live up to everyone's expectations, because we think people won't accept us for who we really are. Once we believe that we are loved and feel secure in our relationships, we stop hiding from others, and we feel the freedom to express ourselves without fear of rejection.

Paul says the fruit of the Spirit is love. One virtue, one attitude, one feeling: love. Then he lists eight more virtues that come from the single source of love: "Joy, peace, patience, kindness, goodness, faithfulness, gentleness and self-control" (Gal. 5:22–23). Jesus collapsed the entire Old Testament teachings into two commandments: Love the Lord your God, and love your neighbor as yourself. "There is no commandment greater than these" (Mark 12:31).

Since this is true spiritually, it is also true emotionally. Love is the parent emotion of all other positive and powerful emotions such as joy, peace, happiness, security, kindness, mercy, and compassion. In the same way, fear is the root of negative, harmful emotions such as worry, anxiety, depression, anger, rage, hatred, and bitterness. But "perfect love drives out fear" (1 John 4:18).

What does "perfect love" mean? The Greek word for *perfect* means "mature."[10] As we grow up in our understanding and in our acceptance of God's love, fear is driven out of our hearts. We are afraid because we doubt God's character and His goodness. We aren't really sure that He is there for us and that He will take care of us. Once we know that God loves us, that He is for us and not against us and will provide for us, we will not be so fearful. I'm not saying that we'll never be afraid of anything again. But we will be more at peace, more confident and calm in the face of life's challenges. We won't overreact to every crisis in life, but with calmness of heart we will know that God will lead and guide us through whatever difficult experience we may be facing.

One night a worried man was pacing the floor, and he woke up his wife. "Why can't you sleep?" she asked.

"Honey, I borrowed one thousand dollars from Bill next door, and I owe it to him tomorrow. But I don't have the money!"

His wife jumped out of bed and called the neighbor on the phone. "Bill," she said, "you know that thousand dollars my husband owes you? Well, he doesn't have it! Good night."

"Now," she told her husband, "you go to bed and let him worry about it."

Unlearn What You Learned

Remember, we are born with only two fears: the fear of falling and the fear of loud noises. All other fears are learned through some experience. We learned to be afraid, and we have to learn how not to be afraid. All the negative, fearful programming we received growing up has to be unlearned. We have to correct our thinking in order to be free from fear. Fear is in the mind as much as it's in the heart. We think fearful thoughts, and that's why we feel afraid. We think about what might go wrong, and then we start worrying about the worst possible scenarios.

Some fears are real and based on real threats to our security. Fear is a normal and justifiable response to the threat of danger. We are anxious about our economy, and rightly so. We have a national debt in excess of $15 trillion, and it is rising and spiraling out of control.[11] Our government thinks the only solution to everyone's problem is to borrow more money. We all know what debt does to us personally, and we all know what it will do to our nation. People are afraid today about our economy because of the real financial threats to our nation.

Most of our fears, however, are imaginary. They are based on our imagination about what might go wrong and what problems may come our way. Let's look back at the promise that Paul gave to Timothy. He told him that besides a spirit of power and of love, God has given us a spirit, or attitude, of self-discipline (2 Tim. 1:7). This is the only time that this Greek word (*sophronismos*) is used in the entire New Testament. The word comes from the Greek root *sophron*, which means "safe in mind."[12] It means the ability to control, to master, and to get a grip on anxious, worrisome, and fearful thoughts. That's what we really need—we need to save our minds from imaginary thinking about every possible thing that might go wrong in life and to start imagining all the great things that can go right with life. When we are children, we use the power of imagination to be anyone we want to be—a superhero, a world champion, or a superstar. But when we become adults, we use the power of imagination to defeat ourselves. Can you remember some of your childhood imaginations? Do you remember pretending to be someone great or that you could accomplish something amazing?

I remember seeing the movie *The Invisible Man* as a boy. The film scared me at first, but then I started thinking about how cool it would be to be invisible. So I dressed up as the Invisible Man and played that role for an entire day. I also saw a movie on Charles Lindberg and his transatlantic flight of the *Spirit of St. Louis*. Afterward I took a big cardboard box that my father had around the house and used it to create a cockpit, drawing all the dials and controls inside and writing "Spirit of St. Louis" on the outside to make it look just like the plane I had seen on TV.

I was seven years old the night I sat watching TV with my family, spellbound as the Beatles performed their first live debut on *The Ed Sullivan Show*. I'll never forget the songs the band performed in that historic 1964 telecast: "I Want to Hold Your Hand," "All My Loving," "She Loves You."[13] After the show was over, I made a guitar out of cardboard and string, and I dreamed of playing guitar. (I play the guitar to this day.)

What are some of your childhood imaginations? Can you remember those exciting times as a kid when you pretended to be someone other than yourself? Learn to use that power of imagination again to dream of all the wonderful things you can do and accomplish in life. We cannot master life until we first master our thinking. When we master our minds, we will master our fears.

Here's a powerful principle from the Bible: "Take captive every thought to make it obedient to Christ" (2 Cor. 10:5). Instead of allowing fear to take us captive and make us its prisoners, we need to take the imaginations of fear captive to wholesome thinking—to make our fearful thoughts obedient to Christ. What does that mean? It means to submit our fears to the promises that Jesus has given every one of us who call Him Lord.

When fear tells you that you will lose everything, make it obedient to God's promise that He will supply everything you need. When fear tells you that you are alone, make it obedient to God's promise that He will never leave you or forsake you. When fear tells you that you will get sick, make it obedient to God's promise to heal you. When fear tells you the future is bleak, make it obedient to God's promise to fulfill His purpose. When fear tells you nothing will work out for you, make it obedient to God's promise that He will work out everything for your good.

Did you know that eighty times in the Bible God specifically says, "Fear not"? Jesus told a man named Jairus who was worried about his very ill daughter, "Don't be afraid; just believe" (Luke 8:50). We need to live by those five words: *Don't be afraid; just believe!* In the same way that we learn to be afraid, we can change our thinking and unlearn the fears that haunt us.

God desires that we live in perfect peace as we trust Him. Freedom begins with discovering the hidden fears that hold us back and then taking the fearful thoughts captive, making them obedient to God's promises. For every fear we face, God has a promise we can believe that will defeat that fear.

Face Your Fears

Fear is a persistent enemy. It won't go away by itself. We have to stand up to our fears and do the thing we are afraid of in order to break free from our fears.

I delivered my first sermon at the age of fifteen. Our church was having a youth Sunday, and the young people were leading in all the elements of the service. The youth group selected me to preach, although I hadn't told anyone that I was going to be a preacher. I think they were used to me speaking my mind about things, so they thought I would do a good job preaching a sermon—but I didn't know the first thing about how to write a sermon, much less deliver one. To this day I don't know why I didn't decline the offer.

I can tell you this: that sermon was a masterpiece. I know that because my mother wrote it for me! Or at least she helped me write it. She selected the passage for the sermon. It was Matthew 6:25, "Do not worry..." Fitting words for the occasion, I'll have to admit. I still remember the surge of panic that rushed through my body when I woke up on that Sunday morning. Words fail to describe the terror I felt as I awaited the moment I would speak before the whole church family.

I met the pastor in his study before the service. I told him how nervous I was, and he tried to console me by telling me about a great preacher—D. L. Moody, I think—who preached his first sermon at fifteen. His words didn't help me. I thought, "Well, Moody was an idiot too for letting someone talk him into it!" I wanted to run out of the church and never come back. What if I failed? What if I embarrassed myself? What if people made fun of me? All those "what-ifs" rushed through my mind. But I had to learn to face my fears.

Nervously I waited through the singing, the offering, and the special presentations. Then my moment of destiny arrived. The pastor introduced me and invited me to bring the sermon. I walked to the pulpit with great fear and trembling. I opened my Bible to Matthew 6 and started to read. Then I prayed—something like, "O God, help!" (That's the prayer I was praying in my head that the people didn't hear.) Then I started to preach. When I did, something incredible happened. The tension and terror left me, and suddenly I felt confident. I felt at home behind the pulpit sharing the Word of God with the people. The bondage of fear was broken the moment I did the thing I was afraid of doing. The same thing will happen to you when you face your fears. Don't run away from your fears; run toward them, and they will fall before you, defeated by your faith.

The best way to confront our fears is to ask, "What is the worst thing that can happen? What can I do to prevent the worst thing from happening? What options do I have if the worst thing happens?" When we ask and answer these questions, we will master our fears. Now ask, "What's the best thing that can happen? What can I do to make the best thing possible? What will I do to celebrate the best thing when it does happen?" Then we'll have our minds focusing on the positive and not the negative. Here's a principle that has helped me to deal with my fears and not be controlled by them: control what you can control, and leave the rest to God.

Remember the adage: "Fear knocked at the door. Faith answered, and there was no one there." As we saw earlier, faith in itself can't eradicate fear—only love can do that. But faith gets our eyes off our fears and onto the truth of God's promises and the greatness of His power.

Jewish people are taught this simple prayer: "Father, into

Your hands I commit my spirit." Sound familiar? It's the prayer that Jesus prayed from the cross as He was giving up His life as a sacrifice for our sins. We need to pray this same prayer and surrender our fears to God. "Father, into Your hands I commit my _____."

What do you need to put in that blank? What fears, worries, and anxieties do you need to surrender to God today? When we give up our fears, we will gain God's peace. What a fantastic deal!

One day a father took his two grade-school children for a river ride in a pontoon boat. As they were going up the river, suddenly the boat's motor stopped. When the father looked to see what was wrong, he suddenly noticed that the red sweater his daughter had been wearing was tangled up in the propeller. Then his son yelled, "Sherry fell in!" In horror the father saw his little girl tangled up in the propeller. She was submerged just beneath the surface of the water, staring right at him, holding her breath. He jumped into the water and tried to pull the motor up, but it was too heavy. Time was running out.

Desperately the father filled his lungs with air and dipped below the surface, blowing air into his daughter's lungs. After giving her air three times, he took a filet knife and cut the red sweater from the propeller and lifted Sherry into the boat. Although she had survived, her cuts and bruises needed medical attention, so they rushed her to the hospital. When the crisis was over, the doctor asked the little girl, "Why didn't you panic?" She said, "We've grown up on the river, and our father taught us that if we panic, we'll die. Besides, I knew my father would come and get me."[14]

Give up your fear, and gain the perfect peace that only God gives when we trust Him completely.

Chapter 7

DON'T LET ME DOWN

Dealing With Disappointment

THERE IS A story about the devil auctioning off all the devices he had used against humanity. A man who was at the auction noticed an old worn-out dagger, and he also noticed that it was very expensive. Intrigued, he asked the devil why the dagger cost so much, since it seemed worn out and useless. "That is the most effective device I have used against humanity throughout history. That's why it's costly. It's the dagger of disappointment."

A business executive fails to get the job promotion she expected.

A newly married couple fails to qualify for their first home mortgage.

A teenager fails to make the high school football team.

A young man is shattered as his fiancée breaks off their engagement.

A pastor struggles with a declining membership.

A doctor grieves that he could not cure a patient.

A couple faces the news that they are unable to bear children.

We've all felt the dagger of disappointment stab our hearts. We know the feeling of dissatisfaction that comes from unfulfilled dreams, unreached goals, and unmet expectations. We get disappointed in people: we thought we could count on someone, but that person let us down. We get disappointed with situations: we thought things would all work out, but they fell apart. "Life's not fair," we complain. We get disappointed with God: He failed to answer prayer the way we expected Him to. We have faith and expectation in His power and grace, but circumstances did not work out as we had hoped. We get disappointed in ourselves, and this may be the biggest disappointment of all: we set goals and fail to reach them. We make promises but fail to keep them. We know our potential and yet, at times, we fall short of what we know we could be and do in life.

Disappointment is the gap between our expectations and our achievements. If we graduate from college and expect to make four thousand dollars a month in income but end up with a job in our field making only twenty-five hundred dollars, we are disappointed. Disappointment doesn't have anything to do with our circumstances. In this case, for example, many people would be happy with twenty-five hundred dollars a month. Disappointment is based on what we expect to get in life. The wider the gap between what we expect to happen in life and what actually happens, the greater the disappointment.

Disappointment comes from unanswered questions. We wonder why the innocent suffer but the guilty thrive. We start off with the dream of a happy marriage only to see the relationship end in divorce. We raise our children in a healthy environment, but still they rebel against everything we taught them. We make financial plans and save up money for college or retirement only to see a bad economy sweep it all away just as the ocean tide takes away the sand on the beach. Life's disappointments can leave us angry with God and cynical toward life.

Disappointment can lead either to depression or to a new decision to move forward with life.

Singing the Blues

Asaph, the music minister for King David, wrote Psalm 73 at a low point in his life. He started off the song on a positive note, saying, "Surely God is good to Israel, to those who are pure in heart" (v. 1). But then his disappointments poured out in the lyrics that follow. He said, "But as for me, my feet had almost slipped; I had nearly lost my foothold. For I envied the arrogant when I saw the prosperity of the wicked" (vv. 2–3). Those who had no regard for God were living the high life, while he was at rock bottom. He wrote, "When I tried to understand all this, it was oppressive to me" (v. 16). Does life ever seem oppressive to you when you consider your disappointments?

Asaph felt like he was getting a raw deal from God. He even started thinking that it was pointless to trust God. "Surely in vain have I kept my heart pure; in vain have I washed my hands in innocence" (v. 13). He made the mistake of thinking that because he was a man of faith, his life would be free of problems. He made the mistake of connecting his faith to his circumstances. Then, when his circumstances went sour, he gave up his faith in God.

We get disappointed because we put our faith in the wrong things. We need to learn to put our trust in God and nothing else. Circumstances change—we go through good times and bad times. People change—sometimes they come through, and sometimes they let us down. The only One who never changes is God. He is the only real constant in our lives.

We will be disappointed if we put our faith in anything other than God Himself. Asaph nearly lost his faith because he measured the faithfulness of God by his circumstances. Your faith is going to be put to the test. Life's difficulties do not refine our character; they *reveal* our character. Fortunately Asaph discovered four powerful truths about God that helped him overcome his disappointment:

> Yet, I am always with you;
>> you hold me by my right hand.
> You guide me with your counsel,
>> and afterward you will take me into glory.
>> —PSALM 73:23–24

Then he goes on to offer one of the most personal prayers found in the Bible: "Whom have I in heaven but you? And earth has nothing I desire besides you. My flesh and my heart may fail, but God is the strength of my heart and my portion forever....But as for me, it is good to be near God. I have made the Sovereign LORD my refuge" (vv. 25–26, 28).

Asaph found out that when he was near to God in prayer, life began to make more sense. His questions were answered. His perspective was changed. His complaints gave way to gratitude. Whatever our situation, we can trust God, because "we know that in all things God works for the good of those who love him, who have been called according to his purpose" (Rom. 8:28). That doesn't mean that everything in life is good. It's not! Many things that happen to us are bad experiences. But God works in all things for our good.

The Great Chicago Fire occurred in 1871. Historians estimate that as many as three hundred people died, and tens of thousands were left homeless.[1] One of the heroes of the Great Chicago Fire was an attorney named Horatio Spafford. Spafford lost a lot of his real estate in the fire, which caused him great financial loss. Yet he helped others who had been made homeless by the fire. Because of his generosity and service, Spafford was well known throughout Chicago as a true Christian.[2]

A couple years after the fire, in November 1873, Spafford and his family decided to take a vacation. Spafford was a good friend of the evangelist D. L. Moody, and his family decided to meet Moody on one of his evangelistic campaigns in England and then travel from there to Europe. But before they were to leave for their trip, Horatio was unexpectedly detained by business concerns in Chicago. His wife, Anna, and their daughters went on ahead to England, with the plan that Horatio would later join them. But the ship on which the family was traveling collided with an English sailing vessel and sunk within twelve minutes. Anna Spafford was one of the few passengers who survived. Tragically, all four of Horatio and Anna's daughters were among those who died.[3] Anna Spafford's heartbreaking telegram to her husband read: "Saved alone. What shall I do."[4]

Horatio immediately set sail for England to join his wife. As his ship passed by the location where his daughters had drowned, Horatio Spafford penned these words:

> When peace like a river attendeth my way,
> When sorrows like sea billows roll,
> Whatever my lot, Thou hast taught me to say,
> "It is well, it is well with my soul."[5]

Like Asaph of old, Horatio Spafford found peace in the presence of God. His disappointment was balanced by the presence of God. Following these great tragedies, Horatio and Anna had three more children—a son who died of illness when he was young and two girls who lived full lives. The family went to Jerusalem to do benevolent work among Jews, Arabs, and Christians. Their daughter Bertha gave us the story behind the song: the music to Horatio's words was composed by Philip Bliss, and the musical score was named after the ship that was lost at sea.[6]

I once spoke with a young woman who was brokenhearted. The man she had wanted to spend the rest of her life with in marriage moved out of town, got a new job, and ended his relationship with her. She poured out her heart: "I can't eat. I can't sleep. I have no goals in life. I can't concentrate on anything." Suddenly she stopped and said, "Listen to me. I sound like a country song." That's what disappointment does to us—it turns into a country song.

GET REAL

So how do we shake off the dust of disappointment and get on with the business of living? We need to face the fact that life is imperfect. People are imperfect. The government is imperfect. Jobs are imperfect. Churches are imperfect. Schools are imperfect. Most importantly, *we* are imperfect, and all this adds up to a lot of disappointment. Disappointment comes from our unrealistic expectations.

Take a good look at your expectations and ask yourself if you are being real or if you are living in a fantasy world. Perfectionists live in the biggest fantasy world of all. They expect themselves and everyone else to be perfect. That fantasy thinking makes them—and everyone else—miserable and sets them up for constant disappointment.

You ask, "Are you telling me that if I expect less, I will not be disappointed?" No, I'm not telling you to expect less, but I am saying that you should be realistic in your expectations—and that may mean expecting less at times. If we just expect less in general, we'll become pessimists, and that's certainly not the cure for disappointment. We simply need to get real in our expectations of God, others, and, yes, ourselves. It's our unrealistic expectations that are the root cause of our disappointments.

I hear people say, "I can't believe this is happening to me! Why me?" Why *not* you? Do you feel you are exempt from the issues of life? Do you think you are different from everyone else or that you have special favor? The fact is, everyone goes through the same struggles in life. "No temptation has seized you except what is common to man. And God is faithful; he will not let you be tempted beyond what you can bear. But when you are tempted, he will also provide a way out so that you can stand up under it" (1 Cor. 10:13).

Why would any of us expect that our life experiences would be any different from everyone else's? We all go through the ups and downs of life. We all go through joy and sorrow, success and failure, triumph and tragedy. We all go through times of abundance and times of lack. We've all had great jobs, and we've all been fired. We all have stories of answered prayer and unanswered prayer. The point is, get real. It will help you deal with life as it really is, not as you wish it were. You know the pop saying, "It is what it is." I like to add, "It is what it is—get used to it." We have to take the good with the bad and deal with life on its own terms. Then we can defeat our disappointments before they defeat us.

Have you ever behaved out of character and then said, "I can't believe I acted like that"? Sure, you have. We've all done that. But why are we shocked at ourselves when we behave certain ways? That only shows how unaware we are of our own weaknesses. Disappointment comes out of overestimating our strengths and underestimating our weaknesses. Again, these are unrealistic expectations of ourselves.

One time Jesus took His disciples to a garden to pray with Him. He was facing the most challenging moment of His life: the cross. He prayed, but His disciples fell asleep. He woke them up and asked them to pray with Him. Again they fell asleep. Jesus knew the challenge facing Him and them. But they were totally unaware that He was about to be arrested and that their lives would be in danger also. They thought they were strong enough to face the challenge.

Jesus told His disciples something that we all need to learn: "Watch and pray so that you will not fall into temptation. The spirit is willing, but the body is weak" (Matt. 26:41). When Jesus was arrested, the disciples all deserted Him and ran for their lives. Just like those disciples, we don't always conquer our weaknesses; sometimes our weaknesses conquer us. We say yes when we had vowed to say no. We yield when we had resolved to stand our ground. We surrender when we had been determined to fight. We run away when we had promised to stay. The spirit indeed is willing, but the body, with all its vices, is weak.

D. L. Moody said, "I have had more trouble with myself than with any other man I've met."[7] Paul the apostle said the same thing:

> My own behaviour baffles me. For I find myself not doing what I really want to do but doing what I really loathe.... I often find that I have the will to do good, but not the power. That is, I don't accomplish the good I set out to do, and the evil I don't really want to do I find I am always doing. Yet if I do things that I don't

really want to do then it is not, I repeat, "I" who do
them, but the sin which has made its home within me.

—ROMANS 7:15, 18–20, PHILLIPS

Paul was real with himself. Even though he met Jesus in a
vision and even though he remains one of the most powerful
and influential ministers of all times, he was in touch with his
weaknesses. Such honest self-awareness frees us from unrealistic expectations of ourselves. And here's something interesting: when you face and accept your own weaknesses, you will
be more accepting, less demanding, and more realistic in your
expectations of others as well.

Why do we look in a mirror when we get up in the morning?
It would be a lot easier and faster for us if we showered quickly,
got dressed, and headed off to face the day. It's looking in the
mirror that slows us down. So why do we do it? We look in
the mirror to become aware of the things that we cannot see
about ourselves otherwise. Just as we need to look into a natural
mirror to see what we look like physically, we need to look into
a spiritual mirror to see what we look like internally.

A mirror forces us to get real with ourselves. We may think
we look great or that the clothes we are wearing look cool or
that we're in great shape, but when we look in the mirror, we
have to get real. I don't mean that we should look in the special
mirrors they put in hotels or dressing rooms that make people
look taller and thinner! We need a real mirror that tells the
real story. Once we see ourselves as we are and get real, we can
then accept ourselves, and we can free ourselves from constant
disappointment.

STAY POSITIVE

Disappointment tends to make us negative and cynical. We cop a bad attitude about the future because we are disappointed with the present. If we can't forgive ourselves and others for the past, we won't have a future. It takes mental discipline to lock disappointment in a closet so that it doesn't influence our entire life. It takes mental discipline to be grateful when we're hurt, hopeful when we're aching, and joyful when we're discouraged. If you don't take charge of negative, toxic thoughts and feelings, they will take over your life.

The greatest battle we fight is the battle for the mind. When you are disappointed, find something you can look forward to in order to counterbalance your disappointment. Stop reading right now, and complete this sentence: "Today I am looking forward to _____."

Disappointment is about the past and the present, so we need something in the future to occupy our thoughts so that we don't obsess over our disappointments.

When Jesus went to the cross, He sang a song of praise! Talk about mental discipline! He was looking past His suffering to His resurrection and to the salvation of the world. "For the joy set before him [he] endured the cross" (Heb. 12:2). When we have something joyful set before us, we can endure anything. It is the joy that we have set before us that carries us through disappointments to a new start. If we don't constantly have some joy set before us, then we are going to focus on our disappointments. Goals help us get going, while disappointments make our lives come to a grinding halt.

The question is not "What disappointment have you experienced?" The question is "What goals have you set before yourself that fill you with joy, hope, and expectation?" The question is not "What bad thing happened to you?" but rather "What have you set before yourself today that will carry you from disappointment to expectation?" What's in front of you is more important than what's behind you. Don't look back—keep looking forward.

Charles Boswell was a football star at the University of Alabama with high hopes of a professional football career. However, during World War II he lost his eyesight in combat. So instead of playing football, he went on to become a blind national and international golf champion. The lesson of his life is: never count what you've lost but what you have left.[8]

Check Your Motives

Have you ever been disappointed in your relationships with others? If so, it would be a good idea to consider what motivates you in your relationships. In the psalm of Asaph that we looked at earlier (Ps. 73), Asaph had to check his motives in his relationship to God. He said that he had kept his heart pure for nothing. He said that his faith in God and his service for God had meant nothing. He was envious at the prosperity of the ungodly. Asaph's initial response of disappointment is much like that of people today. Much of what is taught today about faith is little more than how to childishly manipulate God in the same way we as children learned to manipulate our parents.

A lot of the disappointment we deal with in life comes from our futile efforts to control others. We can be very subtle in our manipulations with others—so much so that even we ourselves are often unaware that we are manipulating those around us. When people don't respond to our control and we don't get what we want from them, we get frustrated and disappointed. We use money, privileges, and promises to control. This is a big issue for parents with adult children. Parents have a hard time accepting their children as adults. When children become adults, their parents have to change the way they relate to them. If they don't, they will have serious friction in their relationships with each other.

Let love be your only motivator, and don't expect anything in return. Then you won't be disappointed. The power of unconditional love is the ability it gives us to do what is right with no expectations of others. Jesus even told us, "Give to everyone who asks you, and if anyone takes what belongs to you, do not demand it back....Love your enemies, do good to them, and lend to them without expecting to get anything back" (Luke 6:30, 35). What powerful words: "Don't expect to get anything back." You gotta be kidding me!

No, Jesus was not kidding, and He was not speaking symbolically. He meant exactly what He said. He was showing us how to free ourselves from demands and expectations that lead to disappointment. We're not disappointed because someone let us down; we're disappointed because we expected something back from that person. Unconditional love gives, serves, and helps others for the pure motivation of concern for them, not to get something back from them. We can apply Jesus's words to so many areas of our relationships. Do everything in love and because of love.

Let It Go

I have a friend who was manipulated by a con artist. This trickster convinced several people that he had a lot of money from the sale of a multimillion-dollar business that was tied up by the government. He told his sad, incredibly unbelievable story to everyone he could. People bought into the scam and gave this man money for an expensive mortgage, private tuition for his daughter, and the payment of all his bills. This went on for several years and finally came to a tragic end when people realized he had conned them.

My friend had loaned this man fifteen thousand dollars for a few months until the presumed "release of funds" would enable him to pay everyone back. When the date on which the man had promised to repay people arrived, he, of course, used a "The check is in the mail" routine. This went on for three months, until my friend finally realized there was no money.

So my friend gave up on ever collecting the funds. He never asked the man for them again, even though he still ran into the man who had taken him for fifteen thousand dollars. He never got the money back. I asked him if he was angry about it. He said, "No. And the reason I'm not angry is that I made a policy for myself years ago that I would never loan money that I could not afford to lose. It has always been my policy to not expect anything back if I loan money to someone. That way I am never disappointed."

That's a great policy to have, and it's one that lines up with what Jesus taught. When you give something, loan something, do a favor, help someone out, then do it in love and out of love without expecting to get anything back. You will discover the joy of helping others, pure and simple, and that becomes your reward. Furthermore, God will see what you do and why you do it, and He will reward you. Jesus said, "Your Father, who sees what is done in secret, will reward you" (Matt. 6:4).

Make this your own prayer today: "Find rest, O my soul, in God alone; my hope comes from him" (Ps. 62:5). It's all the other expectations that disappoint us. Wait for God alone, no one else and nothing else, and keep your expectation only in Him, and you will shake off the dust of your disappointments.

Chapter 8

DON'T LET THE SUN GO DOWN ON ME

Driving Out Anger

ONE OF MY favorite Elton John songs is "Don't Let the Sun Go Down on Me." It reminds me of a spiritual truth: "'In your anger do not sin': Do not let the sun go down while you are still angry" (Eph. 4:26).

Winston Churchill said, "A person is about as big as the things that make him angry."[1] I have come to the place at which I believe anger is a useless emotion. Anger may have some small value when it motivates us to do something good—to make a change or to stand up for justice. But even then we can have more positive motivations for doing things than being mad. Anger hurts us personally, and it damages our relationships.

I have thought a lot about the meaning and the implications of this scripture: "Man's anger does not bring about the righteous life that God desires" (James 1:20). Anger works against everything God desires for us. Anger undoes what God is doing in our lives. We all get our feelings hurt, and we tend to stay mad about it. But anger works against us living the best life we can live. It doesn't produce anything valuable on its own. The products of anger are often harsh words, retaliation, and broken relationships.

We will always get angry. Anger is a natural, healthy emotion. Yet it is the most difficult emotion to manage. When we're angry, we often lose perspective, and we also lose control of our words and our actions. The longer we stay mad, the bigger mess anger makes in our lives and in our relationships.

Anger will not go away by itself. It's like tea—the longer it steeps, the stronger it gets. When we keep anger inside, it builds in intensity until we blow up in rage. Unresolved anger is like a volcano building in power until it erupts. When it blows, it unleashes far-reaching, devastating effects. When our anger gets the best of us, we say and do things that we regret and that we can't undo. It's hard to repair the collateral damage done after an angry outburst.

Understand Your Anger

Anger is a feeling of displeasure caused by a real or an assumed wrong. It is usually caused by "what happened to me." It ranges from irritation to rage. Anger is a feeling that we have in response to threats against us. It also comes from our desire to gain control of a person or a situation. Anger is often based on our exaggerations of what others have done to us. We want to strike back and get even.

Three types of anger can be identified. First, *impulsive anger* is a way that we fight for self-preservation and is a hasty reaction to anything that threatens us. Second, *internalized anger* lies beneath the surface; it is deep-seated resentment that builds up within us over time. Third, *intrinsic anger* is so constant that it becomes a character trait of irritability, moodiness, and sullenness.

Spiritually it is important to know that anger is not a sin, but it can lead us into sin if we don't resolve it. "In your anger do not sin" (Eph. 4:26). It is clear that anger and sin are two different things and that we can be angry and not sin. In fact, 375 of the 455 uses of the word *anger* in the Bible refer to God's anger. I can understand and appreciate God's anger toward us in certain situations, because every parent knows that our kids can drive us crazy at times. God's anger is pure and holy, not like our anger, which is often out of control and destructive. Anger impairs our ability to think clearly and to control our behavior. We can also understand anger as being either passive or aggressive. Here are the symptoms of passive anger that psychologists have identified:[2]

+ *Secretive behavior:* giving the silent treatment, muttering under the breath, avoiding eye-contact, putting people down, gossiping, anonymous complaints, stealing

+ *Manipulation:* emotional blackmail, pretending to be sick, sabotaging relationships, using a third person to report negative feelings, using money to control people

+ *Self-blame:* apologizing too often, being too critical of yourself, inviting criticism from others

+ *Self-sacrifice:* being overly helpful, refusing help, soaking in the praise, having a martyr complex, doing with second best, setting yourself and others up for failure, underachieving, irritation toward little things while ignoring serious issues

+ *Detachment:* lack of passion and interest, giving the cold shoulder, sitting on the fence while others make decisions, looking unconcerned,

deadening emotions with substance abuse,
spending inordinate amounts of time with
machines or objects or intellectual pursuits,
talking about frustrations but showing no
emotion

+ *Obsession:* keeping things too clean and orderly,
habitually checking on things, over-dieting
or exercising, demanding everything be done
perfectly

+ *Evasiveness:* turning your back to a crisis,
avoiding conflict, not arguing back, becoming
paranoid that others are talking about you or
plotting against you

Now, let's take a look at the symptoms of aggressive anger:[3]

+ *Threats:* frightening people with what you might
do to them, finger pointing, wearing clothes with
violent images, road rage, slamming doors. I met
someone who told me that her nickname at home
as a teenager was "Door Slammer."

+ *Harm:* abuse, breaking confidence, profanity,
ignoring people's feelings, willfully discriminating, labeling people negatively, name-calling

+ *Destruction:* throwing things, destroying objects,
sabotaging a relationship, reckless driving, substance abuse

+ *Blaming:* accusing people for your own mistakes, blaming people for your feelings, making general accusations

+ *Hyperactivity:* manic behavior like speaking or walking too fast, working too much and expecting others to do the same, driving too fast

+ *Showing off:* grandstanding, expressing mistrust, not delegating, being a sore loser, wanting to be in the limelight and on center stage all the time, not listening, talking over people's heads, expecting a simple apology to fix everything

+ *Selfishness:* ignoring others' needs, not responding to requests for help, vengeance, always wanting to punish, refusing to forgive, bringing up hurtful memories from the past

+ *Unpredictability:* outbursts, explosive rage over minor things, giving out unjust punishment, inflicting harm, use of alcohol and drugs, illogical arguments

That's a heavy list. It illustrates how pervasive anger is and how destructive it is when we don't have a handle on it.

WHO'S PUSHING YOUR BUTTONS?

One of the first steps in dealing with anger is to not let it get out of control. We need to build in some self-controlling steps so that we don't end up in a place in which we explode and lose control. Once we get to the boiling point, it's too late to do anything about our anger. Learning to keep a lid on our anger is the first and most important step in managing it.

That means you have to know your "buttons." Buttons are those things—whether people, topics, or situations—that you tend to easily get angry over. Some people know just how to push your buttons. What are the things that make you angry? What situations irritate you? Who are the people who rub you the wrong way? It's important to know yourself and the things that push your buttons.

Once you know what things upset you, you can do two things to control your anger and to develop more self-control. First, avoid the things that make you angry. Don't put yourself in provoking situations. Second, if you can't avoid those kinds of situations (and people), then mentally prepare yourself before walking into those circumstances. Give yourself a pep talk. Tell yourself not to fall into the trap of anger. Don't overreact to the things that upset you. Don't take things too seriously. If you prepare yourself mentally, you won't get caught off guard, and you will be able to keep a lid on your anger, frustration, and irritation.

The most important lesson in dealing with anger is to learn not to get angry so easily. Get to the place at which things don't make you so irritated or mad. Start overlooking things that now bother you. Laugh at some of the things that generally irritate you. Slowing down your anger response time is the best way to handle anger. Psalm 37:8 states, "Refrain from anger and turn from wrath; do not fret—it leads only to evil."

Here's some great advice: "Do not be quickly provoked in your spirit, for anger resides in the lap of fools" (Eccles. 7:9). Solomon in his wisdom doesn't tell us not to get angry; he says don't get angry *quickly*. Slow down! When we overreact and get angry too quickly, we end up speaking and acting thoughtlessly. "A quick-tempered man does foolish things" (Prov. 14:17).

God is slow to anger, and we should follow His example (Exod. 34:6). Love "is not easily angered" (1 Cor. 13:5). Love does get angry, but it is not *easily* angered. Two of my favorite psalms are about the anger and mercy of God. God's "anger lasts only a moment" (Ps. 30:5), but "his love endures forever" (Ps. 100:5). God gets angry, but His anger only lasts a moment. His mercy, however, lasts forever!

What a contrast, and what an example for us who say we want to be godly. I am so tired of hearing the word *godliness* used by religious people who think that it means being narrow-minded or following petty rules and religious traditions. Godliness means being like our heavenly Father, whose anger lasts only a moment but whose mercy lasts forever. Mercy, not anger, should be our response to others.

The apostle James tells us to be "quick to listen, slow to speak and slow to become angry" (James 1:19). When we look at the sequence of those three statements, we discover a formula for keeping our cool. First, we should be quick to listen. This will keep us from overreacting and misinterpreting what people say to us. Second, we need to be slow to speak. If we slow down our words, we will slow down our anger. Then, third, it follows naturally that we will be slow to become angry. We may still get mad at times, but our anger will be much more under control. It will be appropriate to each situation instead of being an immediate, out-of-control outburst. We will find out by experience that it is impossible for people to yell at us when we are whispering to them: "A gentle answer turns away wrath, but a harsh word stirs up anger" (Prov. 15:1).

Now that sounds great, but what do we do when we are past

the point of slowing down and we've already become angry? What do we do then? Let's take some of the earlier lessons we've learned and apply them to managing anger. We shake off the dust of anger when we do three things: Get it out. Get over it. Get on with it!

Get It Out

Absolutely the worst thing you can do with anger is to keep it in. When we bottle up our anger, it troubles our thoughts and our feelings. Eventually we will either explode with an angry outburst and say or do things we will regret, or our anger will come out in passive-aggressive ways. Either way, hidden anger will work its way out and wreck everything in its path. Anger only stays hidden so long: "An angry man stirs up dissension, and a hot-tempered one commits many sins" (Prov. 29:22).

It's best for us to express our anger in constructive, healthy ways rather than to wait for anger to find its own expression. Dr. Laurence Peter, educator and writer, said, "Speak when you are angry—and you'll make the best speech you'll ever regret."[4] Hidden anger is much like an infection in the body—it needs to be treated immediately and removed from the body before it causes great harm.

You can "get it out" by telling God in prayer how angry you are. Some of the psalms in the Old Testament are about as gut-level honest as a person can get. The psalmist pours out his anger and disappointment at times and even asks God to judge his enemies. I don't think God answers those prayers, but I think they help to get our anger out. Once we get it out, our emotions settle down, and we are able to think more clearly. It's then that we ask God to bless those who curse us and that we pray as Jesus did: "Father, forgive them, for they do not know what they are doing" (Luke 23:34). But we really can't pray that and mean it until we first get out our anger.

Another way you can get your anger out is by writing down your thoughts. Keeping a journal is a great way to keep your emotions from getting bottled up. Don't tweet your anger! What you write will be read by the world, so keep a personal journal where you can vent your thoughts and feelings. Once you get your feelings out, they won't trouble you so much. You can go back later and read what you wrote, and you can see how far you have moved on from the feelings you had. You will also be glad you got your feelings out in private and didn't act on them.

Finally, you can get your anger out by addressing the person with whom you are angry. You may need to sit down with them face-to-face and tell them how you feel. At some point you have to get in touch with your anger, as uncomfortable and risky as it is, and tell that person, "I am angry with you about what you did, and I want to resolve it." If you are going to do this, you need to make sure that your goal is to reconcile, not just to vent. Give the person an opportunity to listen to you, and then let the person respond and clarify things to you. You will then know whether your anger is justifiable or is based on a misunderstanding.

The goal of this kind of conversation should be to resolve things. A venting session would escalate into more anger and make matters worse, not better. If you are going to get your anger out with someone, be prepared to accept the person's apology. Be ready also to admit that perhaps you misunderstood the situation. And most of all, be ready to forgive so that you can be reconciled with the person. If you just want to vent your anger, do it in private. But if you want to restore your relationship, go to the person with whom you are upset, share your feelings, forgive, and make peace.

Get Over It

Once you get it out, get over it. The matter is over, and the time for being angry needs to end. If you want a new beginning of peace, you have to put an end to your anger. You can't enjoy the new until you're finished with the old. Old things have to pass away before all things can become new. (See 2 Corinthians 5:17.) There will be plenty of new issues to get angry about in the days to come, and you will need to handle each of those when they arise, so you can't afford to be storing up anger over past issues. Learn to resolve issues and to put an end to them so they don't keep troubling you. Jesus said, "Each day has enough trouble of its own" (Matt. 6:34). We don't have the time or energy to deal with the baggage of yesterday—each day has enough of its own challenges and troubles.

The story is told of two Buddhist monks who were walking in a thunderstorm. The men came to a swollen stream. A beautiful young woman stood at the banks of the stream, wanting to cross, but she was afraid of the current.

One of the monks asked, "Can I help you?"

"I need to cross this stream," replied the woman.

The monk picked her up, put her on his shoulders, carried her through the swirling waters, and put her down safely on the other side. He and his friend then went on to the monastery.

That night his friend said to him, "I have an issue with you. As monks we have taken vows not to look on a woman, much less to touch a woman's body. Back there by the river you did both."

"My friend," said the other monk, "I put that woman down

on the other side of the river. You're still carrying her in your mind."[5]

Let things go. Get over it, and move on.

GET ON WITH IT

Once we get our anger out and then get over it by leaving it in the past, we're ready to get on with our lives. Avoid chronically angry people and learn the way of peace. The Book of Proverbs reminds us, "Do not make friends with a hot-tempered man, do not associate with one easily angered, or you may learn his ways and get yourself ensnared" (Prov. 22:24–25).

Jim Elliot and four of his friends ventured into the land of the Auca Indians in South America in 1956. Barely out of college, they had come to bring the gospel to these people. The Indians, however, attacked the men's camp and killed all five of them. A rescue team arrived later, after the men's wives had lost radio contact with their husbands, and found the bodies in the river and along the beach.

Jim's wife, Elisabeth, continued with her missionary work, and two years after her husband's death she went to live among the Auca Indians. She led the man who had been responsible for the raid against the men to Jesus Christ as his Savior. Today the Auca people are Christians because Elisabeth moved on from her hurt and anger to a new season in her life.[6]

Several years earlier, as he traveled to South America to begin his missionary service, Jim Elliot had written this prayer in his diary: "Make me a crisis man, O Lord; not just a sign-post on the highway of life, but a fork in the road so that men who meet me will come to know Jesus Christ."[7]

Let me close this chapter by offering a prayer for freedom

from anger. Turn your anger over to God, and ask Him to give you the gift of peace.

Lord, I don't want to stay angry. Whether I am justified or not in my anger, I do not want to become an angry person. I forgive those who have hurt me, and I pray for You to bless them. I turn over vengeance to You, because only You can judge us perfectly and mercifully. I ask You to forgive me for lashing out in anger and for not expressing my anger in a healthy way. I choose to be merciful to those with whom I am angry because I want You to be merciful to me. I forgive those who have sinned against me because I need You to forgive me. I release my pain, and I receive Your peace.

I refuse to continue to obsess about this issue that has made me so angry, and I choose to focus my thoughts on living life to the fullest. I refuse to waste another day of being so mad, because this is the day that You have made, and I will rejoice and be glad in it. I ask for Your Holy Spirit to make me better, not bitter, and to produce in me the fruit of love, joy, peace, longsuffering, gentleness, and goodness. As You fill me with Your Holy Spirit, I believe that the anger is being driven out of my heart. I receive Your peace, and I make a commitment to obey Your Word to be a peacemaker—for blessed are the peacemakers, for they shall be called the children of God (Matt. 5:9). In Your name I pray. Amen.

Chapter 9

UNFINISHED BUSINESS

Releasing Resentment

A WOMAN ONCE TOLD me during a counseling session that she was angry with her husband. She blamed him for their financial loss. I asked the woman if she had told her husband that she forgave him. She blurted out, "No, because I haven't!"

I laughed and said, "At least you're honest about it."

Resentment is the most common form of unfinished business. When we are resentful, instead of looking ahead in life we become fixated on people who have hurt us. We want to forgive, but we don't do it, because we don't want to let our offenders off the hook or keep them from being held accountable.

To be resentful is to harbor a grudge, to be unwilling to forgive, or to wish harm or ill will to another as a result of real or imagined injury. The word *resent* comes from the French term *ressentir*. *Sentir* means "to feel," so *re-sentir* literally means "to feel again."[1] When we resent others, we keep on feeling the same hurt, anger, and bitterness of the past. Resentment can make us calloused, fearful, and guarded in our relationships because we don't want to get hurt again. Ralph Waldo Emerson wrote of Abraham Lincoln, "His heart was as great as the world, but there was no room in it to hold the memory of a wrong."[2] How glad is your heart? Is it so filled with greatness that there is no room in it for resentment?

Faith to Forgive

Jesus connected the power of faith to the process of forgiveness: "Therefore I tell you, whatever you ask for in prayer, believe that you have received it, and it will be yours. And when you stand praying, if you hold anything against anyone, forgive him, so that your Father in heaven may forgive you your sins" (Mark 11:24–25). That is a profound statement: "When you stand praying...forgive." Maybe we don't see as many results from prayer as we should because of the resentment in our hearts.

Forgiveness means to forget a matter, to give up our grudges, to absolve of all guilt, and to pardon all sin. That is what God does for us, and it is what we need to do for others. When we forgive others, we are putting our faith in God to work things out for us. We need faith to forgive. Let go of your hurt and trust God to take care of you.

Clogged Arteries

Cholesterol, calcium, and other elements in the body can lead to clogged arteries, which can lead to a heart attack. In much the same way resentment clogs our mental, spiritual, and emotional arteries. Resentment stops the flow of love, compassion, and kindness from us, leaving us with hardening hearts toward others.

There was a woman who was served divorce papers by her husband. He was having an affair with his secretary, and he had decided to leave his wife and their two children to marry the other woman. This woman was devastated. She tried everything in her power to save her marriage, but in time the divorce was final. After months of battling grief and depression, she began to put her life back together. One day she called her ex-husband and invited him and his new wife to her home for dinner. She wanted to tell them face-to-face that she forgave them and that she wanted to release them from any resentment she had held against them in her heart. And that is exactly what she did. She told me that it was an awkward time around the dinner table, but when she forgave them, she felt as if a thousand pounds had been lifted off her shoulders and that she was free to move on with her life.

A lot of people move on after divorce, but they move on angrily. They move on in bitterness. They move on with resentment. It's not enough to move on. We have to move on freed from resentment so we can enjoy our lives. If we don't get free from resentment, we will take it with us and ruin new opportunities and relationships.

When we wreck our car in an accident, we don't just drive away from the accident site. If our car is damaged, we need to get it repaired, because driving a wrecked car on the road is a safety threat to others. In the same way, when we have been in an emotional accident and we are damaged, we don't just move on. We first have to be repaired emotionally. Then and only then are we safe for others to be around. Just as a wrecked car is a danger on the road, wrecked people are a danger to others. Go in for repairs and get your resentment problem fixed; then move on with your life.

GET TO THE ROOT

Scripture is clear on this point of unfinished business: "See to it that no one misses the grace of God and that no bitter root grows up to cause trouble and defile many" (Heb. 12:15). We need to discover and then destroy the root of our resentment. Resentment spills over into our other relationships and negatively affects them. Notice this line in the verse: "See to it that no one misses the grace of God." We need to accept the grace—the unconditional love of God—for us, but then we need to give grace to others.

We often want grace for ourselves but judgment for others. If God is a God of grace and we are His children, then we need to become people of grace. We often think of grace only as a divine quality, but it needs to become the dominant quality of our lives as well. Grace is the answer to resentment. You can't show grace to someone and continue to feel resentful.

Grace means to give freely or to love without condition. Grace doesn't count the cost of its love. It gives without expecting or demanding anything in return. Grace is Jesus praying from the cross, "Father, forgive them, for they do not know what they are doing" (Luke 23:34). He forgave His murderers before He had a chance to get resentful. If we respond to all our injuries and hurts with grace, we won't ever get to the place of being resentful.

The apostle Paul put it this way: "Get rid of all bitterness, rage and anger…along with every form of malice" (Eph. 4:31). Get rid of it. Shake it off. How? He goes on, "Be kind and compassionate to one another, forgiving each other, just as in Christ God forgave you" (v. 32). Shaking off the dust is not simply a passive, personal attitude adjustment in which we just change our minds about how we feel toward others; it is taking action. We go to the people who hurt us, and we treat them with kindness, compassion, and forgiveness. Relationships have to be resolved by action, not simply by a change of heart. We have to do something, not just feel something, in order to get rid of resentment and move on to reconciliation.

The ten Boom family kept and protected Jews in their home during the reign of terror by the Nazis. They built a secret space behind the walls of their house in which Jews could hide when the Nazis performed routine searches. They got away with it for a couple of years and were able to help many Jews escape imprisonment during World War II. Then they got caught. The family members were arrested and sent off to different Nazi camps.

Corrie ten Boon and her younger sister, Betsie, were imprisoned in the infamous camp of Ravensbrück. There the two women suffered abuse, torture, and starvation. Betsie died in the camp. Corrie survived the horrible living conditions and the ever-present threat of death that loomed in these camps of the Nazis.

After the war Corrie traveled, preaching the Christian message of the love of God. After one speaking engagement she was greeted by a man from the audience who had listened attentively to her story of the grace of God. Corrie recognized him as one of the cruelest soldiers who had guarded her and Betsie when they had been at Ravensbrück. Her blood seemed to freeze, and her heart felt cold.

The man said to Corrie, "What you said tonight is true. God does forgive and cleanse us of our sins. Fraulein, will you forgive me too?" Then the man held out his hand to Corrie.

"Jesus, help me!" Corrie prayed.

Corrie wrote, "Woodenly, mechanically, I thrust my hand into the one stretched out to me. And as I did, an incredible thing took place. The current started in my shoulder, raced down my arm, sprang into our joined hands. And then this healing warmth seemed to flood my whole being, bringing tears to my eyes. 'I forgive you, brother!' I cried. 'With all my heart!'"[3]

I watched a recent television interview with Rodney King, the well-known victim of police abuse twenty years ago in Los Angeles. A bystander caught the incident on video, and the ensuing trial for alleged police brutality made national news. When the police were found not guilty of any excessive force, Los Angeles erupted in violence by those who felt justice had not been served. The first question of significance the interviewer asked King was, "Have you forgiven the police who beat you that night in the streets of Los Angeles?"

He responded, "I forgave them a long time ago." He went on to say that the judicial system in America, although slow, works. He said that he was proud to be an American and thankful for the opportunities he has been given by living in this country. And he told the interviewer that the police had gone out of their way to express their regret to him.[4] King could have been an angry, bitter man (with good reason), continuing to tell his story of injustice, but he chose the way of freedom: the way of forgiveness. When we forgive, we set ourselves free from anger and resentment, and we set free those who have treated us unfairly.

SON OR SERVANT?

Jesus told the now-famous story of the prodigal son so that we could understand the love and forgiveness of God. After the prodigal son used up all his inheritance, lost his friends, and ended up with nothing, he came to his senses. He realized what a colossal mess he'd made of his life, and he said to himself, "I will set out and go back to my father and say to him: 'Father, I have sinned against heaven and against you. I am no longer worthy to be called your son; make me like one of your hired men'" (Luke 15:18–19). Why did he make such a statement? Because he didn't think his father would forgive him fully enough to restore their relationship as if it had never been broken. As far as the son was concerned, his rebellion had ruined their relationship for good. Now for the rest of the story:

> So he got up and went to his father. But while he was still a long way off, his father saw him and was filled with compassion for him; he ran to his son, threw his arms around him and kissed him. The son said to him, "Father, I have sinned against heaven and against you. I am no longer worthy to be called your son." But the father said to his servants, "Quick! Bring the best robe and put it on him. Put a ring on his finger and sandals on his feet. Bring the fattened calf and kill it. Let's have a feast and celebrate. For this son of mine was dead and is alive again; he was lost and is found."
>
> —LUKE 15:20–24

Now that's amazing! The prodigal son called himself a servant, but his father still called him his son. There's a big difference between being a servant and a son. A servant has assignments, but a son has authority. A servant is a manager, but a son is an owner. A servant has a job, but a son has an inheritance. The father's forgiveness was so great that it restored his relationship with his son as if it had never been broken. The father restored his son to his original place in the family and to the place of honor that he'd had before he had left home in rebellion. What immortal words: "Let's have a feast and celebrate. For this son of mine was dead and is alive again; he was lost and is found." The son thought about his rebellion, but the father thought only about their restoration.

One day my son David Paul (who was about eleven years old at the time) treated his little sister rudely in the car. Even though she had probably provoked him, he was older than she was, and he needed to learn how to respond appropriately. When we arrived home, I told him to get his Bible, look up Luke 6:31 (the Golden Rule), and write the verse ten times. After that we would talk about what it meant. I thought this would be one of those great teaching moments in life that would shape my son's character.

David went promptly to his room and started writing. After a few minutes I went to check on him. As he sat on the floor writing, I could easily see the agitation on his face. Looking closely, I noticed that the verse he was writing was a lot longer than the Golden Rule. I sat down beside him and asked, "Son, what verse are you writing?"

"The one you told me to write—Luke 15:21," he snapped back. Instead of the Golden Rule, he had written these words from the prodigal son: "Father, I have sinned against heaven and against you. I am no longer worthy to be called your son."

I just laughed, put my arms around him, and said, "Let's just forget about it." So much for a great character-building moment in his life. Then again, maybe he got the point after all. He was my son, and he knew that his father loved him and forgave him.

WHAT'S IT WORTH?

Everyone is investment-savvy today. When we make a financial investment in real estate, stocks, or our 401K, we're looking for a return on our investment. I think of emotions in a similar way—as money that we put into an account. Our emotional investments give us a return. If we invest love, forgiveness, kindness, and generosity into others, we get healthy relationships, personal joy, and a positive response from people. But if we invest anger, resentment, and revenge, then we get depressed, moody, sick, and cynical, and people start treating us in the same derogatory way.

What's it worth to you to stay resentful? What are you getting in return? If you have been resentful for a while, look around you. What do you see going on in your relationships? You will find that your resentment is ruining your life. Is your feeling of resentment and your desire to get even with others worth the return of emotional misery and broken relationships? I don't stay angry for long, and I don't resent people. I get over things quickly and move on, because I realize that the return is not worth the investment. As far as I'm concerned, resentment is a bad investment. Bad financial investments will bankrupt us monetarily, and bad relational investments such as resentment will bankrupt us emotionally.

Two sisters, Jane and June, were bitter, and they hadn't spoken a word to each other for thirty years. But when Jane heard that June was seriously ill, she felt compelled to visit her. From her hospital bed June looked at her sister and said in a faint voice, "The doctors say I'm seriously ill. If I pass away, I want you to know that you're forgiven. But if I pull through, things stay the way they are!" I think it would be safe to say that the return on this relationship was not worth the investment!

GRACE TO FORGIVE

I said earlier that in order to forgive, we need faith. We have to believe that if we forgive others and stop trying to get even with them, God will restore what we may have lost and will provide for us. Well, in order to forgive, we also need grace. You and I need God to give us the determination and the ability to release our resentments to Him and to forgive others. Once we release our resentments to God, we will find it easier to forgive others. If you are struggling to forgive someone and can't let go of your resentment, ask God to help you. He will give you the power to do what you cannot do by yourself. Remember these ten words that can change your life: "I can do everything through him who gives me strength" (Phil. 4:13).

Czeslaw Godlewski was part of a young gang that roamed and pillaged the countryside of Germany after World War II. One day his gang gunned down the family of Wilhelm Hamelmann, killing nine of them. Hamelmann himself was the only survivor. Godlewski served twenty years in prison, but when his sentence was completed, he had nowhere to go, so the authorities kept him in prison. When Hamelmann heard about Godlewski's situation, he asked the authorities if they would release Godlewski to him. In his letter to them, he wrote, "Messiah died for my sins and forgave me. Should I not then forgive this man?"[5]

Robert Frost ends his powerful poem "The Road Not Taken" with these words:

> Two roads diverged in a wood, and I—
> I took the one less traveled by,
> And that has made all the difference.[6]

Time and time again we still stand at the crossroads of resentment and forgiveness, and we will be forced to choose which road we will travel. Take the road of forgiveness, the road less traveled by others but that leads to emotional and spiritual freedom. When we forgive, we are free.

Chapter 10

KNOCKED DOWN BUT NEVER OUT

Pressing Forward After Failure

O NE OF THE first motor skills we learn as infants is walking. When we are young parents, we are so proud to see our children take their first steps. We feel like we're at the Olympics and that our kids have just won a gold medal! We clap; we cheer; we shower them with praise. However, as soon as our children take those first few steps, they fall. We quickly run over to them and help them get back up and tell them how proud we are of them. Then we cheer again when they take another step.

While children go on to learn to walk, in other areas of life it seems that we never get past the first-steps stage. We spend our lives trying to walk, only to fall. We need others to cheer us on and to help us get back up. We also need to run to the aid of others who fall, just as we do with our own children. We need to pick each other up and cheer each other on with every step forward that we take.

When we hear someone say, "If I fail...," we should correct the person and say, "*When* you fail..." The Bible says, "We all stumble in many ways" (James 3:2). But failure does not have to be final. It can be, and should be, part of learning how to walk. Consider the failures of these highly successful people:

+ Thomas Edison failed in two thousand experiments before he finally invented the light bulb.[1]

+ The first time Benjamin Disraeli spoke before the British Parliament, members hissed him into silence and laughed when he said, "Though I sit down now, the time will come when you will hear me."[2]

+ Abraham Lincoln lost several elections for political office and failed in business before finally being elected president.[3]

+ Albert Einstein was asked to drop out of school because he lacked interest in his studies. He also failed an entrance exam to a school in Zurich.[4]

+ In 1932, when Fred Astaire was beginning his career, a Hollywood talent judge wrote on Astaire's screen test: "Can't act. Can't sing. Balding. Can dance a little."[5]

+ When Bob Dylan performed at a high school talent show, his classmates booed him off the stage. Today his songs are more coveted by other artists than those of any other songwriter.[6]

+ W. Clement Stone, successful insurance company executive and founder of *Success* magazine, was a high school dropout.[7]

+ Michael Jordan failed to make the varsity basketball team when he tried out as a sophomore because he was too short.[8]

People who are afraid of failure never risk anything. They play it safe in their dreams, their relationships, their investments, and their careers. People who are afraid of failure miss out on the adventure of life. If you never want to fail or to be hurt, then lock yourself in your house and don't ever come out, because real life means risk, and risk means falling down and getting hurt. But that's OK! When we fall, all we need to do is get back up and take another step. If we fall and stay down, we're done. It's over, and, yes, we will have allowed failure to be final. But it doesn't have to be that way. All we need to do to turn failure around is get back up!

Taking risks doesn't mean being reckless with our choices and decisions. Risk means taking a step of faith into new ventures so that we can experience the best of life. Don't live a limited life. Live life without limits. The fear of failure will keep us from experiencing all that life has to offer. The fear of failure will keep a lid on our potential. The fear of failure will keep our dreams locked inside our minds. We have to take risks to turn our dreams into reality. I like the way this quote I read puts it, "Twenty years from now you will be more disappointed by the things you didn't do than by the ones you did do. So throw off the bowlines. Sail away from the safe harbor. Catch the trade winds in your sails. Explore. Dream. Discover."[9]

The following poem illuminates the power of taking risks.

To laugh is to risk appearing the fool.
To weep is to risk appearing sentimental.
To reach out for another is to risk involvement.
To expose feelings is to risk exposing your true self.
To place your ideas, your dreams, before a crowd is to
    risk their loss.
To love is to risk not being loved in return.

To live is to risk dying.
To hope is to risk failure.
But risks must be taken.
Because the greatest hazard in life is to risk nothing.
If you risk nothing and do nothing, you dull your
    spirit.
You may avoid suffering and sorrow,
But you cannot learn, feel, change, grow, love, and live.
Chained by your attitude, you are a slave.
You have forfeited your freedom.
Only if you risk are you free.[10]

Box Another Round

So what do we do when we fail? To use an athletic metaphor, we get up and box another round! James Corbett was a professional boxer in the late nineteenth century. His unique boxing technique changed prizefighting from a free-for-all to an art form and led to his being called the "Father of Modern Boxing." On September 7, 1892, Corbett won the World Heavyweight Boxing Championship by knocking out famed boxer John L. Sullivan in the twenty-first round. He effectively ended Sullivan's career with his innovative boxing technique that enabled him to stay clear of Sullivan for twelve rounds and eventually to wear him down with jabs. When asked how he became a champion, Corbett said, "I always just told myself, 'Box one more round!'"[11]

The gift of faith is free, but the life of faith is a fight. God gives everyone faith—it's what we do with our faith that counts. The apostle Paul described the life of faith as a fight: "I have fought the good fight, I have finished the race" (2 Tim. 4:7). That's the kind of attitude we need to overcome failure. We have to decide to get back up and fight another round.

Don't Stay Down

When we fail, it is easy for us to become victims of our own devices. The things we tell ourselves and the emotions we experience can keep us down. When we fail, especially morally, the first feeling we experience is guilt. Guilt is a feeling of remorse and regret. It is also a fear of punishment. Guilt is a powerful and positive emotion that leads us to confession, apology, and forgiveness—and change, if we embrace it. But guilt can also be a negative and destructive emotion if we don't seek forgiveness for our wrongdoing and then move on from guilt to grace. Once we gain the forgiveness of those we have wronged and make restitution for any damage we have caused, we need to move on past guilt. Guilt is healthy in the short term but highly destructive over the long haul.

In the Old Testament there is an account of God's people gathering for a time of repentance of their sins. The people listened to God's Word as it was proclaimed by Ezra, a teacher of the Law. They confessed their sins to God and prayed for forgiveness. But then they were depressed. Ezra, aware of what they were feeling, quickly changed the mood of the day and said, "Stop feeling remorse. Let the guilt go. The joy of the Lord is your strength!" (See Nehemiah 8:9–10.) Guilt is only useful as a means of moving us to change. Once we receive forgiveness from God and from others, we need to enjoy it so that we can face life with joy.

Guilt will sap a person's strength. The psalmist David described his feelings this way after his affair with Bathsheba: "When I kept silent, my bones wasted away through my groaning all day long....My strength was sapped as in the heat of summer" (Ps. 32:3–4). So what did David do? "Then I acknowledged my sin to you and did not cover up my iniquity. I said, 'I will confess my transgressions to the LORD'—and you forgave the guilt of my sin" (v. 5).

God not only forgives our acts of sin, but He also forgives the guilt of our sin. Many people accept forgiveness for their actual sins and failures, but they still live with the guilt of those sins. Guilt will keep us in depression and will keep us down so that we don't get up from our failures. But once we receive forgiveness for the guilt of sin and failure, we will have the strength to get up and fight another round, because the joy of the Lord gives us strength.

The second defeating emotion that comes with failure is embarrassment. I have a friend who is going through a divorce she doesn't want. She has kept it a secret from her friends and family, understandably, because she doesn't want the pressure of having to answer probing questions. Whenever she tells me that she is concerned about what people will think or that they will be critical, I remind her that most people are too absorbed with their own lives to worry about hers.

Most people are understanding, loving, and kind—at least the people who matter in our lives are. People on the periphery of our lives who may criticize us, judge us, or gossip about us don't matter. They are not players in the game of our development—they're just people in the stands. In an athletic game the players on a team are all pulling for one another. Each member has the other's back. The people who are the players in our lives, who are on our team, want what's best for us, and they will support us through failure to help us get back up. We should never have to feel embarrassed in front of the team players in our lives.

Finally, failure can make us feel disqualified. I have a friend, a minister, who experienced moral failure. One day I was at a gathering of ministers and overheard a few of these men commenting on my friend's failure. One of them remarked with a harsh, judgmental tone, "Well, I think that when a minister sins, that disqualifies him for good. God can never use a person again once he fails like that." I couldn't help but interrupt and say, "I pray that isn't so."

The prophet Jeremiah was thankful that the mercies of the Lord are new every morning (Lam. 3:22–23). About the time I heard that disparaging remark, I happened to be doing studio-recording work on a solo music project. I had written a song titled "I'm Praying for You" but didn't yet have a second verse. That conversation and the experience of my friend gave me the lyrics I needed for my second verse:

> When I heard today you fell from grace,
> Then someone came along to take your place.
> When people tell you that you won't survive,
> I want to tell you heaven hears your cries.
> And I'm praying for you,
> Every step of the way.[12]

It's not the people who put you down that count. It's the people who are praying for you, who believe in you, and who pick you up when you fall who are important in your life.

SWEET OR SOUR?

We shouldn't blame God for our mistakes or failures, and we shouldn't blame Him for the mistakes and failures of others. "I can't believe that God let this happen!" we often complain. But our actions are not God's fault. Our choices are not the same as God's will. Quite often we are victims of other people's failures—those of our husband or wife, our children or parents, our coworkers or friends. Our lives are just as impacted by the decisions and actions of other people as by our own. We are connected with others, and we should always realize how our actions affect others. Now, with the increase of globalism, our lives are affected by what goes on in the whole world, not just in our own nation. We are often involved in the collateral damage of other people's failures.

We can be victims of other people's poor decisions and failed plans. One person is faithful and devoted in his marriage, but the spouse is not, and the faithful one is hurt by the failure of the other. A person works hard for a company, but the company practices poor business policies and goes bankrupt, and the person ends up out of work. The government passes policies that cause economic recession, and the people bear the brunt of its poor leadership. We have to deal with our own failures but also with the impact of other people's failure.

We can't change what's happened to us, but we can decide how to use it. It has been said that bitterness comes to all. It sours some and sweetens others. We must use it to sweeten our spirit. Failure can be like salt or like sugar, depending on how we use it and apply it to our lives.

Write a New Chapter

Wouldn't it be nice if we could just snap our fingers and undo the decisions we've made that have brought ruin to our lives? Unfortunately we can't. But despite that, we have the power of choice. Things that have been decided can be undecided. We can't undo old decisions, but we can make new decisions that will override and correct old ones.

A young woman I spoke to was anxious about the future and

afraid of making mistakes. She told me, "I don't want to end up saying, 'I could have…,' 'I should have…,' or 'I wish I had done so and so.'" I told her that we're all going to say those things at some point. There is no way for any of us to live without failure, regret, and disappointment. We simply need to limit failure and to learn from it when it happens. Don't waste your failures. Use them to gain wisdom.

I once spoke at a conference for ministers and counselors. As I looked at the schedule, I noticed that one of the workshops was to be conducted by a minister who had authored a best-selling book about ten years earlier. But after he wrote the book, he had experienced moral failure. He went through a restoration period and then became active again in ministry.

I later learned from someone who went to this man's workshop that very few people attended. I couldn't help but wonder if it was because of his failure. At one time this minister would have been a headliner at the conference. Now he was given an afternoon seminar that drew a handful of people. We have this idea that we can learn only from people who we think have their act together. But everyone has failed at some point. We can learn a lot from people who have survived failure.

One of the greatest proofs to me that the Bible is inspired by God is that it records stories of failure. If we had complete editorial authority of the Scriptures, we would have edited out those stories. Noah got drunk after the Flood. King David committed adultery. The apostle Peter denied Jesus. You would think that these men would have told the Bible writers, "Hey, leave that part of the story out. You're making me look bad." But failure is a part of life, and we can gain as much wisdom from failure as we can from success. I'm not glorifying failure or recommending it. I'm just being real with you and reminding you that we all fail. When we do, we need to get back up and become wiser so that we don't repeat our mistakes.

Simon Peter's denial of Jesus is one of the all-time classic stories of failure. Peter denied Jesus three times during the Lord's pre-crucifixion interrogation. Jesus had told Peter that he would deny Him, but Peter didn't believe Him. In fact, at the Last Supper he had told Jesus, "I am ready to go with You to prison and to death. Everyone else may fall away, but not me. I will stand with You to the end." (See Luke 22:33.) But when his hour of testing came, he failed the test, and he denied that he even knew Jesus out of fear for his own life. Peter overestimated his strengths and underestimated his weaknesses.

When the rooster crowed early in the morning as Peter was denying Jesus for the third time, Jesus turned and looked straight at Peter as the words of denial fell from Peter's lips (Luke 22:60–61). Peter ran out of the courtyard and wept bitterly over what he had done. He had denied the one he loved the most. The man who believed Jesus was the Son of God had now claimed that he didn't even know Him. After Jesus was raised from death on the third day, Peter felt that he was disqualified as a disciple, so he went back home and returned to the fishing business. That's where he had been when Jesus had first called him. But when Jesus and Peter met on the beach one day, Jesus didn't mention Peter's denial to him. He spoke only of his future and enabled him to write a new chapter in his life (John 21:1–19).

It's interesting to note what Jesus had told Peter on the night of the Last Supper when He had predicted Simon Peter's denial: "I have prayed for you, Simon, that your faith may not fail. And when you have turned back, strengthen your brothers" (Luke 22:32). Although Jesus had known that Peter would fail and deny Him, He assured the disciple that He had prayed for him and that he would make it through his failure.

People often say, "I just want to start over," but starting over is a myth. I know a person who wanted a divorce in order to purge his marriage of past mistakes so that he could date again and start over. We can't go back and undo anything in our lives—but we don't need to. Starting over is not the answer to our failures. What has happened in our lives is our story, and we're stuck with it. We can deny certain things or pretend that they didn't happen to us. But we don't need to do historical revisionism to our own lives.

Accept the story of your life as it really is. While you can't rewrite the past, you can write a new chapter and determine your future destiny. You can't start over, but you can get a fresh, new start. Past chapters of your story don't have to determine the present or future chapters. You decide where you want to go from here. If you don't like the current story of your life, then write a new chapter. You do not have to let life happen to you. Too many focus on what's happening to them and not on what they are making happen, but you can take charge of your life and change the course you're on.

It's Not What You've Lost but What You Have Left

Failure makes us focus on things we have lost. And loss brings grief. Grief is a feeling of sadness that is associated with the loss of someone or something we love—a loved one, a marriage, a job, valuables, our social connections.

We can get stuck in the place of grief. Our life is put on hold. We become paralyzed in our depression, anger, sadness, confusion, and pain. Now, there is an appropriate time for grief.

Grief is a vital part of life, and it cannot be—nor should it be—rushed by well-meaning people telling us to move on. On the other hand, we cannot afford to let grief be the last chapter of our lives. There comes a time for us to pick ourselves up off the mat and to box another round in the game of life. Decide to stop focusing on what you have lost and think about what you have left. Then take that and start writing a new chapter.

A New Beginning

How can we write a new chapter after we've failed? Let me take you back to the beginning for a minute—to the beginning of time itself. The Genesis story of creation teaches us how to make a new start and write a new chapter.

"In the beginning God created the heavens and the earth. Now the earth was formless and empty, darkness was over the surface of the deep, and the Spirit of God was hovering over the waters. And God said, 'Let there be light,' and there was light" (Gen. 1:1–3). This is not just a story about creation; it is also about re-creation. Look at the dreadful description of the planet in its origin: formless…empty…dark.

Sounds like our lives when we have failed, doesn't it? Those three words may describe the way you feel: Formless—no structure, disorganized, aimless, chaotic. Empty emotionally, spiritually, and physically. In the darkness of depression and hopeless about your future.

But then something incredible happened, and the same thing can happen to you too: the Spirit of God hovered over the waters. That word *hovered* means that God was watching over the formation of the planet and that He was moving with great power to bring about His purpose. God hovers over our lives too. He watches over us.

Then God spoke. Light burst forth. Darkness was dispelled. Chaos turned to order. Emptiness was filled. The old was gone, and the new had come!

Think of the Creation story, which shows us how God works, in comparison with this passage: "If anyone is in Christ, he is a new creation; the old has gone, the new has come!" (2 Cor. 5:17). When we read the Creation account in Genesis, we learn how God will make things new if we will turn over to Him our messes—those things that are formless, empty, and in darkness—and allow Him to make a masterpiece. The seven-day process of creation occurred in three steps—the same three steps we need to take in order to write a new chapter when we have failed or been involved in the collateral damage of someone else's failure. Let's look at them.

1. *Forming.* The first three days of creation describe the forming of the world. In a similar way we need to organize, or "form," our lives by setting goals and planning our days. We must decide where we want to go in this new season and then make a plan to get there. We have to bring organization to the chaos that failure has caused us in order to write a new chapter.

2. *Filling.* During the next three days in the Creation story God filled the skies, the seas, and the land with birds, fish, and animals. Finally, on the sixth day, He made man in His own image. In the same way, once we get our lives reorganized and have new direction, we need to fill our lives with good things—with experiences, relationships, and goals. Meet new people. Get a

new job. Go back to school. Pursue a new career. Volunteer for community service. Get involved in politics. Join a church. Take music lessons. Go to art classes. Fill your life with good things instead of sitting around rehearsing your failures or obsessing over what has been lost.

3. *Finishing.* "Thus the heavens and the earth were completed in all their vast array. By the seventh day God had finished the work he had been doing; so on the seventh day he rested from all his work" (Gen. 2:1–2). God promises to finish His work in us and to never give up His work in us. We too need to commit ourselves to finishing what we start and to reaching our goals. Failure does not have to be final. We may be knocked down, but we don't have to be knocked out. Henry Wadsworth Longfellow wrote, "Great is the art of beginning, but greater is the art of ending."[13]

Michelangelo described his sculpting as the making of men. He called it freeing images from the prison of stone. Instead of trying to fashion a person from stone, he merely chiseled away the excess stone around the already existing image within.[14] He could look at the raw stone and see *David*, the *Piéta*, *Moses*, and *Bacchus*. Sometimes he quit in frustration, as in the case of a statue of Matthew, which he left half finished. According to legend, Michelangelo said that the stone refused the release of the prisoner. He left several others unfinished as well, four of the most famous being his slave sculptures in Florence. Not so with us. Decide to finish what you start. Don't allow failure to stop you from dreaming and pursuing the best life you desire. Don't leave your story unfinished because you have been through a time of failure.

Thomas Edison's plant caught fire one night and was engulfed in flames. He and his family stood by helplessly watching his lab go up in flames. As he watched his life work being destroyed, Edison said, "Although I am over 67 years old, I'll start all over again tomorrow."[15]

Ruth Bell Graham once told a story of several men who spent a day fishing in the Scottish highlands and later sat in a local inn having dinner. One of them got carried away describing the size of a fish he had caught. As he flung out his hands, he hit the cup of tea the waitress had been about to set on the table. The tea splattered on the wall, creating an ugly brown stain. The fisherman was embarrassed and began apologizing when one of the guests at another table jumped up and said, "Don't worry about it." The man pulled a charcoal pencil from his pocket and began to sketch around the ugly stain, and before long there appeared a beautiful royal stag with its antlers spread. The artist was Englishman Sir Edwin Landseer, known for his animal paintings and particularly for the lion sculptures at the base of Nelson's Column in Trafalgar Square.[16]

Close the chapter of failure. Failure is not final. Start today and begin writing a new chapter in your life. You can even turn a mess into a masterpiece.

Chapter 11

I WANT TO BE POSSIBLE!

Overcoming Inadequacy

A STORY IS TOLD of an elementary school teacher who asked her students what they wanted to be when they grew up. The responses echoed through the classroom: "A doctor," said one girl. "A football player," said a boy. "An astronaut," said another. "The president," said a fourth student.

The teacher noticed, however, that one little boy hadn't said a word. "What would you like to be when you grow up, Tommy?" the teacher asked.

Tommy thought for a moment, then answered with one word: "Possible."

"Possible?" asked the teacher. "What do you mean?"

"Well," he said, "My mom is always telling me that I'm impossible. So when I get to be big, I want to be possible!"[1]

All of us, if we're honest about it, want to be possible! The problem is, we feel impossible. Psychologist Alfred Adler, in his theory on personality, pointed out that one of the key motivations we all share is a striving for superiority.[2] We seek power in this way to compensate for a basic sense of inadequacy and incompetence.

Norman Vincent Peale in *Power of the Plus Factor* tells of an incident in which he was walking though the winding streets of

Hong Kong. As he walked, he saw a tattoo shop. In the window were displayed samples of the tattoos available—anchors, flags, mermaids. But what caught his attention was the tattoo consisting of three words: "Born to lose." Curious, he entered the shop and asked the owner if anyone had ever had that terrible phrase "Born to lose" tattooed on his or her body. When the shop owner told him that he had known several people to choose that tattoo, Peale asked him, "Why? Why would anyone do that?"

The shop owner simply tapped his forehead and in broken English said, "Before tattoo on body, tattoo on mind."[3]

You weren't born to lose—you were born to win.

Charlie Brown said to Linus, "The moment I was born and set foot on the stage of life, they took one look at me and said, 'Not right for the part.'"[4] We all struggle with feelings of inferiority and inadequacy from the time we are very young. If we are going to win in life, we have to shake off the dust of inadequacy so that we can rise up to our full potential.

Joshua battled the same feelings of inadequacy that we do. Who in his or her right mind would want to follow Moses? Who could follow an act like that? New leaders often fail when they have to fill the shoes of a great leader who has gone before them. People constantly compare the new leader to the previous one, and the pressure of having to measure up to former standards causes the new person to give up.

To this day Moses is revered. Movies are still made about his life and his exploits. It's no wonder that Joshua felt inadequate at the thought of filling the shoes of Moses. Look at this résumé:

+ Was the greatest Old Testament prophet
+ Was miraculously saved by Pharaoh's daughter at birth
+ Grew up as the son of Pharaoh in the palace
+ Met God at the burning bush
+ Brought God's judgments against Egypt
+ Liberated the Hebrew slaves
+ Parted the Red Sea
+ Received the Ten Commandments in stone
+ Spoke face-to-face with God
+ Saw the glory of God
+ Led Israel through the wilderness
+ Authored the first five books of the Bible

The name of Moses is known around the world and held in honor thirty-five hundred years later. As great as he was, however, Moses was not the one who was called to lead Israel into the Promised Land. Moses was called to get the people out of Egypt. It would be Joshua's responsibility to get the Israelites into their new land. Joshua needed to know that he wasn't called to replace Moses or to fill Moses's shoes—he was called to fill his own shoes. Inadequacy comes from comparing ourselves with others instead of being who we were made to be. The first step to overcoming inadequacy is to stop comparing ourselves with others and to discover our own place in life.

The Comparison Game

Get out of the game of comparing your gifts, talents, abilities, interests, calling, aptitudes, and attributes with other people. It's a game we can't win. If we compare ourselves with the people we admire and look up to, we will always feel inadequate. And besides, people don't want us to do that anyway—they want us to be ourselves. Each of us is unique. There's no one in the world just like anyone else. You and I weren't born to be someone else; we were born to be ourselves and to bring the uniqueness of who we are to this world.

Why do we tell ourselves that we just don't measure up? What are we trying to measure up to? We're not competing against anyone else—we're only competing against ourselves. The only standard we have to measure up to is that of our own potential. Live up to your own potential, not the potential of someone else. Accomplish what you have the ability to accomplish, and don't worry about what other people achieve. Celebrate people's accomplishments, but don't think you have to do the same things.

The real purpose of athletic competition is not to beat our opponent but to beat ourselves. We compete against others because it helps us rise to new levels as we beat our own fears and feelings of inadequacy. In sports we often say that we play to the level of our competition—and it's true. When we play against better athletes and better teams, we get better. We aren't really trying to beat them; we are competing so that we get better.

We don't have to make as much money as our friends do in order to be happy. We have to make as much as we are capable of making and to be fulfilled in the knowledge that we are doing our best. We don't have to live in a house as large as our friends' homes. We have to live in a house that is in line with our own goals and dreams. We don't have to have the same career that our fathers had. We have to find our own way and be our own person in order to be happy and fulfilled.

Instead of measuring yourself by what others have accomplished, measure yourself by what you want to accomplish and by your unique talents, gifts, and abilities. Are you living up to your potential? That's the question you need to ask yourself.

THE COST OF CRITICISM

Feelings of inadequacy often begin in our childhood when we take to heart critical remarks made about us. These can come from a variety of sources: a verbally abusive parent, children who call others names, an awkward experience, a negative label, an ethnic or gender slur, an embarrassing nickname, destructive criticism. Experiences such as these add up to erode our confidence as children and to stifle our potential as adults. Can you remember an experience as a child or a teenager in which you were embarrassed or ashamed? When people made fun of you? When peers ganged up on you? When a teacher embarrassed you? We've all had those experiences that can leave lifelong impressions and rob us of our confidence.

We live in a society of labels. Ethnic labels. Political labels. Religious labels. We tend to stereotype people and to judge them by their labels instead of realizing that everyone is unique. When we are labeled negatively, we can take it to heart and allow that negative label to define who we are. If you have carried a negative label all your life, it's time to shake it off. You have the right and the freedom to define who are. If you were to complete the sentence "I am...," what would you say about yourself? Would you define yourself in a positive, successful way, or have you allowed a negative, defeating label to limit your life?

When we are victims of constant criticism, we develop feelings of inadequacy. But President Theodore Roosevelt put criticism into perspective in his speech "Citizenship in a Republic":

> It is not the critic who counts; not the man who points out how the strong man stumbles or where the doer of deeds could have done them better. The credit belongs to the man who is actually in the arena, whose face is marred by dust and sweat and blood; who strives valiantly; who errs, who comes short again and again, because there is no effort without error and shortcoming; but who does actually strive to do the deeds; who knows the great enthusiasm, the great devotions; who spends himself in a worthy cause; who at the best knows in the end the triumph of high achievement, and who at the worst, if he fails, at least fails while daring greatly, so that his place shall never be with those cold and timid souls who knew neither victory nor defeat.[5]

When we experience numerous failures, we naturally lose confidence. For a young man named Sparky, defeat and discouragement seemed to be commonplace. In first grade he took Valentine's cards to school for every student in the class, but he was so afraid to hand them out that he brought the box of cards home to his mother. He struggled in school, failing eighth grade as well as numerous subjects in high school. He did poorly in sports too. He made the school's golf team, but he lost the only important match of the season and lost the consolation match as well.

Sparky's mother, though a kind woman, was also distant at

times and even overbearing. Sparky didn't make friends easily at school either. During high school he never asked a girl out on a date for fear of rejection. As a young adult he loved a woman (she was the true "red-haired little girl"), but after three years of being with him, she chose to marry another man.

Sparky was a loser. But no matter how many discouragements he experienced, he refused to give up. He knew that he was good at drawing. He remembered how his kindergarten teacher, after seeing one of his drawings, had told him that he'd be an artist one day. As a teenager Sparky drew cartoon after cartoon. His father encouraged him to enroll in a correspondence school that emphasized cartoon instruction, and despite the challenges of the Great Depression, he was able to pay for his son's course. In his senior year of high school Sparky submitted several cartoons to the editors of the yearbook, but his work was turned down. Still, Sparky didn't quit.

After completing high school, Sparky wrote a letter to Walt Disney Studios. He was asked to send some samples of his artwork, so he went to work and spent a great deal of time on them. He sent off his drawings—but one more time he was rejected.

In his early twenties Sparky got a job filling in text balloons for other artists' cartoons. On the side he kept drawing, over time concentrating his cartoons on a group of children he had created. The drawings became somewhat autobiographical and expressed his own feelings of inadequacy and insecurity, particularly in his main character: Charlie Brown. The cartoon character eventually became famous worldwide. Sparky, who had experienced rejection again and again but refused to give up, was none other than Charles Schulz, the creator of the *Peanuts* comic strip.[6] Charles Schulz won his personal battle with inadequacy.

DEMAND MORE FROM YOURSELF

Remember, you and I are God-created, but we have been given the power to make decisions that will shape our future. God's call to Joshua to follow in the footsteps of Moses put a lot of pressure on the young leader, but the pressure forced Joshua to reach higher and to achieve more than he would ever have experienced without the pressure. If we give in to our feelings of inadequacy, we will never reach our potential. Our sense of inadequacy will push us back into a corner and diminish our lives. We need to put ourselves in pressure situations that are demanding intellectually, professionally, educationally, and yes, spiritually, and we will rise to the challenge. You are the most important coach in your own life. Teachers and mentors are important, but each of us has to dig deep and to motivate ourselves to accomplish our goals and live up to our potential.

When God instructed Joshua of old to be strong and courageous, the young warrior took those words to heart. So must we. It's the fearful mind and the inadequate mind that limit our potential. A healthy mind makes the impossible possible and rises to the challenges before us.

We can play it safe if we want to. We can retreat from challenges, pressures, and opportunities, telling ourselves that we can't do what lies in front of us. But if we do, we will miss out on the greatness that God has created within us. You and I need the pressure of challenging situations to bring out the best in us. Don't wait for a challenge to come your way. Find a challenge on your own. Take the initiative to tackle something new, and you will conquer your fears and discover your real power and potential.

I once read a story about a famous pianist who was invited by a friend to attend church. The pianist told his friend, "I will go to church with you if you can take me to a church where I will be tempted to achieve the impossible." Achieving the impossible should be our aim!

I once read a story author Philip Yancey tells about an African safari on which he saw a mother giraffe taking care of her newborn offspring. Shortly after the baby giraffe was born, its mother did something that appeared cruel: she kicked it. Then she did it again. But each time she kicked her baby, the little giraffe got up on its wobbly legs and tried to walk. The mother continued to kick it until finally the little giraffe managed to get up and run away from her kicks.

Philip asked the safari guide, "Why did she do that?"

The guide answered, "The only defense the giraffe has is its ability to get up quickly and to outrun its predator. If it can't do that, it will soon die."[7]

We are like that baby giraffe. We need God to kick us into action. We need our family and friends to kick us into action. We need our teachers and mentors to kick us into action. We need our counselors and advisors to kick us into action. Above all, we need to kick ourselves into action.

SEE YOUR FUTURE, SEIZE YOUR FUTURE

Robert Kennedy said, "The future is not a gift; it is an achievement."[8] Our feelings of inadequacy, however, make us settle for less than we are capable of achieving. God told Joshua, "You will lead these people" (Josh. 1:6). God told Joshua that his future would be to overcome feelings of inadequacy. Leadership is seeing the future and doing what needs to be done to get ready for it. That's what leaders do: they look beyond the present and then help lead people to their future. When we are shortsighted and live only for today, we fail to reach our potential—and we fail to lead others to theirs.

Your future is also the future of the people who are counting on you. If you hold yourself back, you will hold others back. If you rise to your potential, you will lift others up to a new level. Now that truth may make you feel pressure, but you need to feel it. The pressure of being accountable to God and to others motivates us to succeed. We have to make ourselves accountable. Others can't hold us accountable. Holding ourselves accountable is a gift that we give to others because we care about them.

Wall Street Journal reporter Jason Zweig wrote about an interesting set of experiments that suggest that when people are shown computer-aged pictures of themselves—similar to images of missing persons that are artificially aged to provide better guides for searchers—they are more likely to make prudent decisions regarding their future. For instance, they may, he writes, become more diligent about saving money. Having gotten a glimpse of themselves as older people, they can better empathize with their future selves. It is well known that people are less likely to be mean or cruel to someone they can see than to someone they can't (which helps explain the extreme levels of vitriol on the relatively anonymous Internet). Therefore it stands to reason that if you "see" your future self, you might start to regard your future self as a real (if potential) person whose interests you should take into consideration. If so, you will make better, more prudent decisions that extend over time.[9]

Successful people have an ability to visualize exactly what they want out of life and then to stubbornly hold on to their vision—notwithstanding evidence to the contrary. Derek Jeter is the shortstop for the New York Yankees and a ten-time all-star. As a child Jeter was a Yankees fan attending the team's games when he spent summers with his grandparents in New Jersey. Yankees player Dave Winfield inspired Jeter to pursue a career in baseball, and Jeter even predicted in a school essay that he would one day play shortstop for the Yankees. He decorated his bedroom with Yankees paraphernalia and spent his days bouncing a ball off his family's garage door or playing catch with a family member. He was an all-star player in high school.

After high school Jeter was drafted by the Yankees and spent four years in the minors. His first appearance was in a double-header in which he failed to get a hit out of seven at-bats, and he struck out five times. Jeter also made a throwing error, costing his team the game. In fact, in his first fourteen times at bat, he did not get a hit. He batted .202 that season—an extremely low average—and made fifty-six errors at shortstop. Discouraged, frustrated, and homesick, Jeter called his parents daily, racking up $400-a-month phone bills.

But when things got tough, Jeter held on to his goal. He began to work on defense—eight hours a day, seven days a week. Despite the pain and hard work, he kept remembering the words of his parents: "Don't let anyone work harder than you do!" Today Jeter has played eighteen seasons for the Yankees and is a five-time World Series champion.[10]

You too are great at something. It may not be what your parents were great at or what your best friend is great at. You have to discover the greatness that lies within you and then live up to it.

A little boy got a new baseball bat and ball for his birthday. He went to the backyard to hit the ball. He put his bat over his shoulder and said, "I'm the greatest batter in the world!" He tossed the ball into the air, swung, and missed. "Strike one!" he yelled.

He put the bat over his shoulder again and said confidently, "I'm the greatest batter in the world!" He tossed the ball high, swung, and missed. "Strike two!"

His confidence still undaunted, he announced to the imaginary crowd, "I'm the greatest batter in the world!" A third time he tossed the ball high in the air, swung as hard as he could, and missed. "Strike three! You're out!"

Then he said, "I'm the greatest pitcher in the world!"[11]

Once you discover what you are great at, then dedicate yourself to the task of developing that greatness and stop allowing feelings of inadequacy to keep you down.

During World War II the Navy formed a corps of engineers called the Seabees. My father served in the Seabees in the south Pacific. Their motto is "Can Do." We need a "can-do" attitude in order to succeed. Inadequacy will whisper to us, "You can't do it." But we *can* do it if we believe we can.

I guess it was my father's experience in the Seabees and the can-do attitude that caused him to tell me the story of the little train when I was a boy. I can still remember him sitting on the edge of my bed, telling me about this little train that struggled to go up a steep hill. The train kept saying to itself, "I think I can. I think I can. I think I can." As it finally struggled to the top and rounded the crest to begin its descent, it sped down the other side of the mountain saying, "I knew I could! I knew I could! I knew I could!" We have to know we "can do" if we really expect to do something. If we doubt ourselves, who else will believe us?

When Beethoven was threatened with deafness, it is said that he was heard declaring, "I shall seize fate by the throat!"[12] Beethoven first noticed that he was starting to become deaf at age twenty-eight, when he realized he could not hear the church bells from some distance away. By age fifty the great musician was completely deaf. There is a story told about how, in order to better feel the vibrations of its music, Beethoven cut off the legs of his piano and laid the instrument flat on the floor.

He composed the famous "Ninth Symphony" after his hearing was totally gone. The last movement of the symphony is based on the poem "Ode to Joy," which Beethoven loved. Beethoven's composition "Moonlight Sonata" gives a sense of the sadness the man must have felt over losing his hearing, yet despite his loss he continued to bring the world incredible music. He could have given in to his deafness and told himself that he was no longer adequate to compose, but Beethoven "seized fate by the throat" and refused to let his condition stop him.[13]

As we mentioned earlier, psychologist Alfred Adler noted that a driving force in life is the striving for superiority—a sense of adequacy and mastery. Can we master life, or do we feel like game pieces being manipulated by cosmic forces? Can we take charge of our decisions, destiny, and direction, or will we allow circumstances, fears, and doubts to determine how we live?

Here are ten words that will change your life and help you shake off the dust of inadequacy: "I can do everything through him who gives me strength" (Phil. 4:13). I hear athletes quote that scripture often in game interviews. I saw a popular rap artist with those words tattooed across his chest. I even noticed it inscribed on a transfer truck driving down the interstate.

I can do! I can do all things. Not some things. Not just easy things. I can do *all* things. I can handle all things. I can deal with all things. I can face all things with faith, not fear. But here is the secret—I can do this only through Christ who strengthens me. Strength and courage don't simply come from our abilities; they also come from our relationship with God, from learning to depend on His strength and power when our resources are not enough. God won't live our lives for us—that's our responsibility—but He will give us the strength to face life's challenges, difficulties, and opportunities. We will never again feel inadequate when we can say "through Christ who strengthens me."

The Lord has your back. He makes up the difference when you can't measure up. He provides what you lack. When you know where your strength comes from, you will be able to say, "I can do." Take the words *I can't* out of your vocabulary. Live confidently and face what life will bring you today by saying, "I can do everything through him who gives me strength."

Chapter 12

TO THINE OWN SELF BE TRUE

Casting Off Negative Self-Image

Two cows were grazing in a pasture when they saw a milk truck pass by. On the side of the truck were the words, "Pasteurized, homogenized, standardized, vitamin A enriched." One cow sighed and said to the other, "Makes you feel sort of inadequate, doesn't it?"

An identity crisis is the greatest personal crisis every one of us faces. We all struggle with these important questions:

+ Who am I?

+ Where did I come from?

+ Why am I here?

The way we answer these questions determines how we live. Low self-esteem is one of the greatest emotional struggles of our times. This problem is compounded by feelings of guilt and failure. Our self-image is the picture we have of ourselves. Our self-esteem is our sense of worth. We never rise above the view we have of ourselves.

Where does our self-image come from? It comes first and foremost from our parents. How our parents defined us and treated us is the single greatest influence on the way we see ourselves. In many respects, our self-image is merely a reflection of the way others see us and describe us. If our parents were loving, nurturing, and affirming, we grew up with self-confidence and a positive view of ourselves. If, however, our parents neglected us or put us down, telling us that we would never amount to much, then we will tend to see ourselves that way, and we will often fail to reach our potential.

By the time we start going to school, our peers become an even greater influence on us and on the way we see ourselves than our parents are. Peer pressure reaches its height in our teenage years, when being cool and fitting in is one of the most important factors in our development.

Our self-image is also shaped by our experiences of success and failure. When we succeed in academics, sports, music, acting, or a job, we feel confident and have a healthy view of ourselves. When we fail, we lose self-confidence, and we fear taking risks in whatever aspect we have failed.

Genetics plays a big part in our appearance and therefore in our self-image. We inherit our physical features from our parents, grandparents, and other ancestors. We may or may not like how we look, but for the most part we're stuck with ourselves. We can learn to like ourselves—or we can struggle through life.

Culture puts an undue emphasis on physical appearance, and that adds to the stress we feel about ourselves. Cosmetic surgery is a booming industry. People often undergo cosmetic surgery not to improve the way they look to others but to improve the way they look to themselves. Many of the things we do are to manage not our image but our self-image.

Self-image produces self-esteem. If our view of ourselves is positive, we will have a healthy sense of self-esteem. However, if we have a negative view of ourselves, we will suffer with low self-esteem. How do you see yourself? How do you define your-self? What do you think are your strengths and weaknesses? Do you take people's appraisals of you seriously? Do you depend too much on what others say about you? Do you know who you are? Do you have the courage to be yourself? Are you still trying to live up to everybody's expectations? Perception is reality. Seeing ourselves positively is the most important ingredient in developing high self-esteem.

CREATED BY GOD

The theory of evolution is widely accepted today, and that has an effect on the way people see themselves. The first fact of the Bible is that God exists and that He created us in His own image. Think of the difference between the words *created* and *evolved*. Creation involves intention, decision, creativity, design, and purpose. Evolution involves random selection, chance, possibility, probability, and accident. Now people differ as to how they think God created the world, but my point is to emphasize that He did create it, and that gives everything in this universe—including you—significance and purpose.

One day an astronomer made a model of our solar system, showing the planets revolving around the sun. One day a fellow scientist who believed in evolution saw it and commented, "That is a fantastic model of our solar system. Who made it?"

The astronomer replied, "Nobody made it."

His friend said, "What do you mean, nobody made it? Someone had to make it. It couldn't just appear by itself."

The astronomer then seized the opportunity: "Let me ask you something. Why can I not convince you that no one made this tiny model of our solar system, yet you are convinced that the grand design of our solar system from which this model comes happened by itself? By what kind of incongruous logic do you arrive at such a conclusion?"

We have been created by God and in His image. When we recognize that truth, we are in a good place to begin seeing ourselves correctly.

Wonderful Works

One day the psalmist David reflected on the wonder of being created by God. He considered how the hand of God had been working on his development even when he was still in his mother's womb: "For you created my inmost being; you knit me together in my mother's womb. I praise you because I am fearfully and wonderfully made; your works are wonderful, I know that full well.... Your eyes saw my unformed body. All the days ordained for me were written in your book before one of them came to be" (Ps. 139:13–14, 16).

The wonderful works of God are clearly seen during the nine-month journey each of us takes in our mother's womb. Let's consider:

1. *Day One: Fertilization.* The sperm joins with the ovum to form one cell. This one cell contains the complex genetic makeup for every detail of a new human life—the child's sex, hair and eye color, height, skin tone, etc. From that moment on nothing new is added but oxygen, nutrition, and time.

2. *Month One.* The first cell divides into two, and cell division continues as the newly formed individual travels down the fallopian tube to

the uterus. Over five hundred cells are present when this tiny embryo (the blastocyst) reaches the uterus seven to ten days after fertilization. Foundations of the brain, spinal cord, and nervous system are already established, and on day twenty-one the heart begins to beat in a regular fashion with a blood type often different from her mother's. Muscles are forming, and arms, legs, eyes, and ears have begun to show. (The blastocyst is the stage at which many researchers want to destroy the embryo in order to harvest stem cells, which are the building blocks of life.)

3. *Month Two.* By six weeks brain waves can be detected by electroencephalogram, and the brain is controlling forty sets of muscles as well as the organs. The jaw forms, including teeth and taste buds. The baby begins to swallow amniotic fluid, and some have been observed hiccupping. During this time the stomach produces digestive juices, and the kidneys begin to function. Fingers and toes are developing, and at seven weeks the chest and abdomen are fully formed. Swimming with a natural swimmer's stroke in the amniotic fluid, she now looks like a miniature human infant.

4. *Month Three.* Unique fingerprints are evident and never change. The baby now sleeps, awakens, and exercises her muscles by turning her head, curling her toes, and opening and closing her mouth. Even though mom cannot feel the baby move yet, baby is very active. She breathes amniotic fluid

to help develop her respiratory system. The sex can be visually determined and family resemblance may appear as well. By the end of the month all the organs and systems of her body are functioning.

5. *Month Four.* By the end of this month the baby is eight to ten inches in length and weighs about one-half pound. Her ears are functioning and she hears her mother's heartbeat as well as external noises like music. Mother begins to feel the baby's movements, a slight flutter at first that will become stronger. Life-saving surgery has also been performed on babies at this age.

6. *Month Five.* If a sound is especially loud, the baby may jump in reaction to it. Thumb-sucking has been observed during the fifth month. Babies born prematurely at this stage of development often survive, thanks to advances in neonatal medicine. Case in point: Kenya King was born in Florida at nineteen weeks weighing four pounds, eight ounces, and survived.

7. *Month Six.* Oil and sweat glands are functioning. The baby's delicate skin is protected in the amniotic sac by a special ointment called vernix. She grows rapidly in size and strength while her lungs become more developed.

8. *Month Seven.* The baby can now recognize her mother's voice. She exercises by stretching and kicking as she grows even bigger. She uses the

four senses of hearing, touch, taste, and she even looks around with open eyes at her watery home. If the baby is a boy, his testicles descend from the abdomen into the scrotum.

9. *Month Eight.* The skin begins to thicken, with a layer of fat stored underneath for insulation and nourishment. The baby swallows a gallon of amniotic fluid per day and often hiccups. Though movement is limited due to cramped quarters, her kicks are stronger, and mom may be able to feel an elbow or heel against her abdomen.

10. *Month Nine:* Gaining a half-pound per week, the baby is getting ready for birth. The bones in her head are soft and flexible to more easily mold for the journey down the birth canal. Of the forty-five generations of cell divisions before adulthood, forty-one have already taken place. Only four more come before adolescence. In terms of development, we spend 90 percent of our lives in the womb.[1]

The psalmist David saw himself as being a fearfully made, wonderful work of God. He envisioned God knitting him together in his mother's womb. That's an interesting way to describe the nine months of gestation from pregnancy to birth. I don't know how to knit, but I have watched the process take place. The most fascinating knitting I have observed was in the mountains of Turkey where people knitted rugs. Barbie and I bought two rugs from these people and shipped them back to our home in Georgia because we were so impressed with the intricacies of the inspiring images the artists created out of silk. How much more artistic is God's knitting together of your life and mine!

That's why David paused as he considered the wonders of creation and erupted in praise: "I praise you because I am fearfully and wonderfully made." When you consider that you are the unique artistic creation of God, like David you will find great joy in life and celebrate God's wonderful work in creating you. Consider these facts:

+ Our eyes can distinguish ten million colors.[2]

+ Our ears contain twenty thousand hairs that can hear three hundred thousand tones.[3]

+ Our digestive tract is thirty feet long.[4]

+ Stomach acid is one of the most powerful corrosives—it can even dissolve a razor blade. Our stomach grows a new lining every three days to keep from digesting itself![5]

+ Our muscle structure consists of six hundred muscles that if used together could lift twenty-five tons.[6]

+ Our skeletal structure consists of 206 bones. One square inch of bone can withstand a two-ton force.[7]

+ Our circulatory system is sixty to one hundred miles long.[8]

+ Our heart pumps five quarts of blood per minute and two thousand gallons of blood per day.[9]

+ There are one billion red blood cells in two to three drops of blood.[10]

+ Our body grows two hundred miles of capillaries for every pound of body fat that we gain.[11]

+ Our nervous system consists of millions of cells, exceeding the number of stars in the Milky Way. We have thirteen hundred nerve endings per square inch of fingertip that send touch sensations to the brain at the rate of 350 feet per second.[12]

+ Our lungs consist of six hundred million air sacs. We breathe twenty-four hundred gallons of air daily. The surface area of the lungs is one thousand square feet, which is twenty times greater than the surface area of the skin on our bodies.[13]

+ Our brain weighs about three pounds and contains one hundred billion neurons. Each neuron is like a small computer. More than one hundred thousand chemical reactions occur every second in the brain. The brain sends impulses to the body at the rate of two hundred miles per second. The brain stores ten to fifteen trillion memories during our lifetime.[14]

We are fearfully and wonderfully made!

David goes on to consider how God has watched over his life from the time he was conceived. "Your eyes saw my unformed body" (Ps. 139:16). The words unformed body come from the Hebrew word that we translate "embryo."[15] Even before David's body was completely formed, it had all the genetic code needed to become a full human being.

Then David thought about his divine destiny by writing "all the days ordained for me were written in your book before one of them came to be" (v. 16). He knew that he was no accident, no afterthought, no random act; he was the work of God.

A powerful and positive self-image starts when we realize that we are fearfully and wonderfully made. Stop complaining about yourself and instead celebrate yourself. Stop putting yourself down and start lifting yourself up.

In God's Own Image

Of all that He has made in this world, humanity is the height of God's creative work. Only we are made in the image of God. We are higher than the animal kingdom—stamped with the image of God.

On one occasion some religious leaders tried to trap Jesus in His words. They wanted Him to say something treasonous against the Roman government so they could have Him arrested. They asked Him, "Should we pay taxes to Caesar or not?"

Jesus asked for a coin, which someone handed to Him. Holding up the coin, He asked them, "Whose image is on the coin?"

"Caesar's," they replied.

Then came His now famous words: "Then give to Caesar what is Caesar's, and to God what is God's" (Luke 20:25).

But here is the follow-up question: "Whose image is on you?" When we realize that we are stamped with the image of God, then we will render our lives to God as our Creator, Father, and Savior.

Genesis tells us that God created us in His own image and likeness. But what is the image of God?

We are made in the *mental* image of God. As we saw earlier, the first words God spoke to Adam that we know of began with "You are free" (Gen. 2:16). We are free to think, to decide, to reason, to choose, and to act. Animals act on instinct, but humans act on choice. The course of our lives is not predetermined or predestined—we are free to choose and to decide our own destiny. Destiny is not a matter of chance but of choice. Our destiny is the sum total of our important decisions. If you want to know your future, just look at the decisions you are making today, and that will tell you where you are going. You are free!

We are made in the *moral* image of God. God created us with a conscience—that inner voice that tells us the difference between right and wrong. Conscience makes us feel good when we do what is right and guilty when we do what is wrong. The law of God written by Moses on tablets of stone was first written on our hearts. (See Romans 2:14–15.)

We are made in the *social* image of God. God said of Adam when He created him that it was "not good for the man to be alone" (Gen. 2:18). That statement remains true to this day. God created Eve to keep Adam straight. Men are lost in this world without women to help keep them in line. Why did God create Adam before He created Eve? Everyone knows that we make a rough draft before we create a masterpiece.

All joking aside, we have a need for close, meaningful relationships. A healthy life depends on healthy relationships with our family and friends. We have a need to belong to a community that gives us identity, purpose, and significance.

Finally, we were made in the *spiritual* image of God. We

are eternal beings housed in temporary bodies. The Book of Ecclesiastes tells us that God has put eternity in our hearts (Eccles. 3:11) and that when we die, our bodies return to the dust from which they came, and "the spirit returns to God who gave it" (Eccles. 12:7). The apostle Paul described death by saying, "To be away from the body" is to be "at home with the Lord" (2 Cor. 5:8). We are created for a relationship with God—to know Him, to experience Him, and to converse with Him. God walked with Adam in the cool of the day in the Garden of Eden, and He desires to walk with us.

OF MICE AND MEN

Lucy is the name given to what are believed to be the earliest remains of a hominid that were discovered in Ethiopia. Only 40 percent of the skeleton was found. Lucy is speculated to have been three feet, eight inches tall and to have weighed sixty-five pounds. She is also presumed to have had a small brain. The skeleton is the size of a chimpanzee. Lucy is believed to have walked upright and is dated to have lived 3.2 million years ago.[16] In the fall of 2009 news circulated that a new discovery had been made of a skeleton named Ardi. Ardi, also found in Ethiopia, was thought to have lived a million years before Lucy.[17]

A year later scientists were disputing that claim and questioning what kind of creature Ardi was altogether. I noticed something interesting in the articles I read on this subject. First, the words *questions, doubts,* and *disagreements* appeared often to describe the differing views scientists have of skeletal remains. Such words hardly describe any hard, cold facts of science. An Associated Press article noted that the skeletal remains of Ardi "didn't look much like today's chimps, our closest living relatives, even though it was closer than Lucy to the common ancestor of humans and chimps."[18]

Now it is interesting to me that these skeletal remains are not called our ancestors but rather "the closest common ancestor of humans and chimps." There's a big difference between the presumed hominids of Lucy and Ardi being humanity's closest ancestor (that we know of) and actually being an ancestor—a subtle but significant play on words. Humans and chimps have as much in common as mice and men.

Regardless of how many skeletal and fossil remains we find and seek to interpret, there is and always will be a fundamental difference between an ape and a human. Evolution is wrong on one key point—that one species can evolve into another species. No scientific evidence supports the idea that one species evolves into another species. Species can adapt, change, and, yes, evolve within the confines of their species. But that's where science ends and speculation begins. Species have boundaries that keep them within their own kind. God designed everything He created with the ability to adapt to the earth's environment for its survival. If we couldn't adapt and change, we could not survive. But adaptation is a far cry from the blind suggestion that one species, and in this case an ape, evolved into another species when we can clearly see the fundamental differences between an ape and a man. The only thing that humankind and animals have in common is their Creator. "All things were created by him and for him...and in him all things hold together" (Col. 1:16–17). Science, genetics, and the fossil record support the Genesis account that all things reproduce "according to their kinds" (Gen. 1:25).

Divine Design

We are God's masterpiece, fearfully and wonderfully made. The apostle Paul said, "We are God's workmanship" (Eph. 2:10). The Greek word for "workmanship" means "poem" or "work of art."[19] Art is so inspiring. I will always remember my first visit to the National Gallery of Art in Washington DC as a teenager. I was awestruck by the majesty of the paintings and sculptures that I saw. I had seen many of these pieces of art only in books, but to stand face-to-face with them and see the intricate wonders and graphic, lifelike detail of the painter's brush and the sculptor's chisel was breathtaking.

How much grander is God's work of art in creating us in His image. Take a look at David's song of creation:

> When I consider your heavens,
>   the work of your fingers,
> the moon and the stars,
>   which you have set in place,
> what is man that you are mindful of him,
>   the son of man that you care for him?
> You have made him a little lower than the heavenly
>   beings
>   and crowned him with glory and honor.
> You made him ruler over the works of your hands;
>   you put everything under his feet.
> —Psalm 8:3–6

What is mankind? That is the question of our times. Who are we, and why are we here? The psalmist doesn't leave this question unanswered. God is a master artist, and we are the work of His fingers. We are made a little lower than the angels and crowned with glory and honor. We are made to rule in life and to be ruled by nothing or no one but God Himself. When you feel that you don't matter or that your life has no significance, read Psalm 8 and remember who you really are. Your feelings of low self-esteem will have to surrender to the fact that you are crowned with glory and honor. You have the power to rule in life.

One of the greatest moments of my life is the day my first child, David Paul, was born. I had to get past the trauma of being in the delivery room with Barbie during her labor, but the moment Barbie delivered our son and the nurse put him in my arms, I was overwhelmed emotionally. I looked at my son's face, and it looked just like mine. I felt this incredible surge of love for him. The image of my face in his caused the words "God made man in his own image" to echo in my mind. I too had created life in my own image. The God who created me had given me the power to create in my own image. I imagined that the love I felt for my newborn son was the same kind of love that God feels toward us, His children.

God made us to be rulers over all the works of His hands. Are you ruling, or do you feel like life is running over you? Are you taking action to fulfill your potential, or do you feel like a pawn on a chessboard? Think about this phrase: you are God-created but self-molded. Your life is God's gift to you; what you do with your life is your gift to God. He gives each of us our own raw, undeveloped talents and abilities, but we choose how to use those gifts. He expects us to do our very best with them (2 Tim. 2:15).

After God created the world, He said it was good, and then He stopped creating new people, plants, animals, and natural resources. He put us in charge. He told us to be fruitful, to multiply, and to produce something with our lives that will make the world a better place. God put us here to replenish what is lacking, to subdue what is out of control, and to rule over that which is chaotic. What God told Adam and Eve to do He is telling us to do with the resources He has given us.

God gave us the first garden, but He expects us to grow our own gardens. God gave us the natural resources and the intellect to discover and to develop the resources He put in the earth. God did not build the house you live in or design the car you drive or make the clothes you wear. Everything you enjoy was built by the hands of men and women. God created the gold and the silver, but we have to mine these precious stones and make them into beautiful jewelry that can signify our love for someone else.

God created the trees, but we have to cut them down in order to construct houses, churches, and buildings. God created iron, steel, and ore, but we have to mine them, melt them, and mold them into structures, supports, and frames. When God put Adam and Eve in the garden, the Genesis story says He put them there to "work it and take care of it" (Gen. 2:15). You determine your future based on what things you work and take care of.

I once read a story about a tired father who sat down on his couch and turned on his TV after a long day of working and driving in traffic. He started to relax, when his high-strung kindergarten-age son jumped in his lap and said, "Come on, Dad. Let's play."

Thinking fast about how he could occupy his son so he could get a few minutes of rest, the father noticed an ad with a picture of the earth that took up a full page in the newspaper. "Let's play a game," he told his son. He took a pair of scissors and cut up the picture of the earth to create a jigsaw puzzle. He gave the boy some tape and said, "Tape the world together." He imagined this would take his son a while.

The boy was elated over the game and ran to his room with the pieces of paper and the tape. But he came running back to his dad in only fifteen minutes with the picture complete! "How did you do that so fast?" the father asked.

The boy turned the page over. "Look, there's a picture of a man on the back. When I put the man together, the whole world came together."[20]

When we put ourselves together, we will be amazed at how much of our lives and our relationships will come together. Once we fix the world within us and shake off the dust of inadequacy and a negative self-image, the world around us will come together as well. The world around us often mirrors the world within us.

You are fearfully and wonderfully made. You are crowned with glory and honor. You have been given dominion to rule over life's circumstances and situations. Get yourself together, and your whole world will come together.

Chapter 13

IT'S NOT THE END OF THE WORLD

Rejecting Rejection

YOU ARE TURNED down for a date. You are denied a loan. You submit a manuscript, only to have it rejected. You get fired from your job. Your spouse files for divorce. You submit job applications, only to have them returned. You try out for the team but don't make the final cut. You compete for an acting part, only to lose the competition. You apply for the college of your choice but are denied entrance.

Rejection is one of the most painful emotional experiences. New research shows that rejection even causes us physical pain and discomfort. The word *rejection* comes from the Latin word *rejectus*, meaning "to throw back."[1] We have all felt emotional pain when a person or a group of people reject us for some reason.

I have a friend who is in the process of being approved for a kidney transplant. It is a lengthy ordeal to become approved and then to find a donor whose kidney will match the recipient's. The biggest concern in an organ transplant is whether the body of the person receiving the organ will accept the transplanted organ or reject it.

Or consider the rejection of our peers. Do you remember when you were in elementary school and had to pick teams for kickball on the playground? There were two captains, usually the biggest and toughest kids in the class. Then the captains took turns choosing team members. You didn't want to be the last person standing. If you were the last one picked, you weren't really chosen.

Rejection is a painful feeling of not being wanted, loved, or appreciated. I recently talked with a man in his mid-fifties who'd had a successful career in information technology, only to be laid off and forced to search for work in another field. A much younger person replaced him at the company because he required a lower salary, having less experience. This man was unemployed for two years before he found another job in his field, and even then he earned a fraction of what he had made before. A lifelong career was ended for corporate profit.

A close friend of mine told me about someone who had taught in the music department of a Christian college for twenty-two years. His house was on the college campus. Out of the blue he was retired. He never saw it coming. The college planned a big celebration for his years of service, which only poured salt in his wound. I'm sure this teacher would rather have had his job than a going-away party.

Rejection can make us question ourselves. We may start to doubt ourselves. We tell ourselves that we don't "have it" anymore. We may feel unloved or unappreciated. We certainly feel undervalued and that people no longer recognize or appreciate our contribution, effort, and performance.

LOVESICK

Rejection from a love relationship is the most painful form of rejection. It starts early in life. You pass a note to a girl in the second grade: "I like you. Do you like me? Check yes/no." You dread getting the "no" box checked. Love brings with it a lot of anxiety. We wonder and worry if someone will love us back to the extent that we love him or her. If they don't, we feel rejected. When I was in second grade, I had a crush on Suwanee Goram. On Valentine's Day all the students exchanged Valentine's Day cards and candy at school. I told Suwanee that I was going to come to her house that night with a Valentine's Day gift. She didn't believe me. I still recall being a nervous wreck as my father drove me over to her house. I went up to the door and rang the doorbell. When Suwanee's father opened the door, I was shaking like a leaf in the wind, and I asked if she was there.

When she came to the door and I gave her a box of chocolates, I felt like a thousand pounds had been lifted off my shoulders when she smiled and said, "I can't believe you came." The couple of minutes we talked on her front porch brought huge relief from my anxiety. It was nice not to be rejected.

Thirty years ago I met my wife, Barbie, on a blind date. (It's the only blind date I have ever had, and look how it ended up!) I was living in Los Angeles at the time and had come back to Atlanta for two weeks to hang out with my best friend and to meet his new fiancée. My friend's fiancée, Julie, worked with Barbie at Coca-Cola. When I met Julie, she told me, "I have a friend you have to meet."

Julie worked it out for me to call Barbie and to ask her to go on a double date with her and Paul. She assured me that Barbie would say yes. You never want to ask someone out on a date if you're not sure about what answer you will get. You have to do your homework so you don't get turned down. I called Barbie at work and asked her to go to dinner with us that night, and she gladly accepted.

I have a running video in my mind of the moment I laid eyes on Barbie. She walked up a set of stairs from her apartment to my friend's car. She was the most beautiful woman I had ever seen. She was wearing a bright yellow blouse with dark blue jeans and high heels. When she got in the backseat of my friend's car, I immediately moved to the center of the seat to sit closer to her.

We had lunch together the next day. Then on Sunday we were supposed to meet at church—and Barbie stood me up! I called her apartment over and over again, but she didn't answer the phone. I pined away all afternoon and even wrote my first love song for her that day.

That afternoon at about five o'clock I drove over to Barbie's apartment and knocked on her door (it's called stalking today). I just had to see her. The feeling of being stood up on a date or of being rejected was more than I could stand, since I was already deeply in love with her.

(Now you're probably thinking right now, "This guy's a psycho." Maybe so, but I was in love, and love will make a person do crazy things.) Fortunately Barbie let me into the apartment and made up some excuse about having forgotten that we were supposed to meet at church and going instead to the pool. Years later she told me the truth: I was overwhelming her, and she was trying to get some space.

I saw her the next day, but she was getting ready to drive home to Florida for a vacation. I would be going back to California the next week, so if Barbie took her full vacation, I would never see her again. I pleaded with her not to go. I begged her to stay in Atlanta so I could see her some more. (Yeah, I know, more psycho-like behavior.) But she left anyway.

I was lovesick. I couldn't eat, drink, or sleep. Barbie was all I could think about. There were no cell phones or e-mails in those days, and I didn't have Barbie's phone number. I was wasting away with the feeling of rejection. I remember thinking how stupid I had been to let myself get so attached to her. She was too pretty for me, too classy, too everything. She was definitely out of my league.

Then, to my utter shock, Barbie cut her vacation short and drove back to Atlanta. She called me and told me she was back, and she asked me if I could come over to her apartment. "Come over?" I thought. "I'm going to set a NASCAR speed record getting there!" The moment I saw her, I hugged her and kissed her, and that was the beginning of our life together. Four days later, before I flew back to Los Angeles one morning at six, I asked Barbie to marry me. I figured that I had better close the deal before I went back to California. Strike while the iron is hot! To my surprise she said yes. I had known her for eleven days.

We got married nine months later, but I would have married Barbie the day I met her. Being loved is the greatest feeling in the world. On the other hand, rejection is the worst feeling in the world. I can still feel the anxiety I experienced during those first eleven days of knowing Barbie, wondering if she would check the yes box or the no box on the advance of my love.

Closed Doors

I battled a lot with rejection after my college graduation. As a brand-new minister I tried to schedule speaking appointments at churches and only got two engagements in six months. I worked a construction job in Atlanta and also played lead guitar with my brother Tim in a cover band for Top Forty hits. I made contacts with churches and even had my pastor send a personal letter of recommendation to churches. Every door I knocked on was closed.

Then in October of that year, nearly six months after graduating, I got an opportunity to be a youth minister at a church in Birmingham, Alabama. I went there and got off to a great start. Unfortunately, within six weeks I was fired! I went back to Atlanta dejected. I later found out from a leader in the church where I'd worked that the pastor had been jealous of me and wanted me out of there. I learned not to take the rejection to heart. I was hurt but not angry.

I let my disappointment go and made a decision that I have lived by ever since: I would keep moving forward. "Shake off the dust and move on" is my motto. Life is too valuable and opportunities too plentiful for us to get bogged down over disappointing experiences. I want to enjoy every day that I have and not waste a single minute languishing in hurt, anger, and depression.

Jesus Himself said, "I have placed before you an open door that no one can shut" (Rev. 3:8). Eventually we all find an open door of opportunity. Don't let closed doors defeat you in your dreams. For me the door of opportunity opened later that fall after I lost my first job. I had an opportunity to move to California to become a minister. I walked straight through that open door and shook off the dust of getting fired in Alabama, and I bought a one-way ticket to Los Angeles.

At that point in my life I had never traveled out of the southeastern United States. I arrived in Los Angeles with no agenda, and I had no idea what I would do or where I would live. I lived there for a year, traveling all over beautiful California and speaking in a different church every week. I never had a permanent residence. I stayed in hotels, motels, and host homes.

The only mountains I had ever seen before moving to

California were the Blue Ridge Mountains. Don't get me wrong; the Blue Ridge is beautiful in its own right, but the Blue Ridge Mountains look like hills compared to the mountains of the West. I marveled at California's diversity. I could be on the snow-capped mountains above Upland in the morning and be at the sunny beaches of Orange County by the afternoon. Driving through the Napa Valley filled with picturesque wine vineyards was so peaceful. And the thousands of flowers in full bloom in Solvang before they were gathered and then exported around the world was one of the most magnificent sights I have seen in my life.

You know, I would never have gotten to live in California and to enjoy an adventure of a lifetime unless I had been rejected in Birmingham. Looking back on it, I'm glad the pastor fired me. That man gave me an amazing opportunity as a young college graduate. Now that I think about it, I never did send him a thank-you card. Getting fired didn't discourage me or make me want to quit. It motivated me to shake off the dust and get moving. When a door slams in your face, move on as quickly as you can in pursuit of the open door of opportunity that's just around the corner.

We need to handle rejection the way Jesus did: "Christ suffered for you, leaving you an example, that you should follow in his steps.... When they hurled their insults at him, he did not retaliate; when he suffered, he made no threats. Instead, he entrusted himself to him who judges justly" (1 Pet. 2:21, 23). I like that statement—"He entrusted himself to God." That is the secret to shaking off the dust of rejection. Commit yourself and your life to God, and look to Him to provide for you, to defend your cause, and to protect you from the painful experiences of life.

People will eventually let you down. I don't say that as a cynical commentary on humanity—we *all* let people down at times and are let down by others. Jesus entrusted Himself to God because only God is perfectly trustworthy.

Guard Your Heart

Don't let rejection make its way into your heart, and don't take rejection personally. You have to guard your heart and mind against the pain of being unwanted. When someone rejects you, don't allow the experience to define who you are. People's rejection of you is a commentary on who they are, not on who you are. You always have the freedom to define yourself.

Proverbs reminds us, "Guard your heart, for it is the wellspring of life" (Prov. 4:23). A wellspring is the deep underground spring of water that supplies a well. The proverb is telling us to protect our hearts from feelings of hurt, anger, and disappointment, which can turn the waters of our lives bitter. We want the fresh water of faith, hope, and love to be flowing out of our lives. Keep the wellspring of your heart pure, and don't allow rejection to contaminate the water of your soul.

You can't control what people do or say—you can only control how you respond. You certainly can't stop people from rejecting you, but you can stop it from affecting you. Shake it off and move on. Rejection is like poison. Don't swallow it—don't allow it into your system. If you take it into your heart, it will destroy your confidence and make you retreat from new adventures. Instead of going forward with your goals, you will draw back in defeat. Instead of rising up to new levels, you will settle for the status quo. Instead of taking on new challenges, you will seek the comfortable option of keeping things the way they are.

REJECTION MAKES US STRONGER

Rejection makes us stronger and better able to face the challenges and disappointments of life. Rejection toughens us up. Howard Barker, dramatist and playwright, said, "I submit all my plays to the National Theatre for rejection. To assure myself I am seeing clearly."[2]

Highly successful people bounce back when they are rejected. They get up and go again, and with each rejection they face, they become stronger and more resolved to try things again. We decide whether rejection makes us or breaks us. Rejection cannot faze us if we don't allow it to go to our heads or get into our hearts. Shake it off and come back stronger.

Rejection can make us reevaluate ourselves and our work. Maybe there is something we can learn from being rejected or from having a project we have worked on rejected. Maybe it will help us better ourselves. Don't waste the painful, disappointing experiences of life. We can gain wisdom through even the most difficult moments we face.

PUT IT IN PERSPECTIVE

Perception is reality. Being rejected is not the end of the world. Don't blow your hurt out of proportion and make a bigger deal of it than it is. I'm not minimizing the pain you may be experiencing, but I am encouraging you to take a step back and put things into perspective. You're still standing! You still have options. You have new opportunities coming your way, and you may miss them if you're blinded by bitterness.

One of the worst forms of rejection is divorce. A husband or a wife who is divorced by his or her spouse feels rejected. The children of divorce often feel rejected as well, and they sometimes think they are to blame for their parents' breakup. I have a friend whose wife recently filed for divorce. His first wife had died of a debilitating disease, and he was by her side during those years of suffering. As I encouraged him through the divorce proceedings, my friend told me that dealing with divorce was worse than living through the death of his first wife.

Affairs are rampant today. An affair is an act of betrayal that destroys the trust a couple shares. It is almost impossible for a married couple to survive an affair. Even when there is forgiveness and both the husband and wife work hard to rebuild their relationship, the memory of the affair looms in the background, casting a shadow of doubt over the solidarity of the marriage. The victim of the affair feels rejected, wondering why he or she was not good enough for his or her spouse.

The only way we can handle life's disappointments is to put them into perspective. We have to be able to make some sense out of things in order to handle them. We can't change the things that have happened to us, but we can change the way we look at those things. Instead of seeing ourselves as victims of rejection, we need to see ourselves becoming better as a result of what has happened to us.

How can we put rejection into proper perspective? One of the most important principles in viewing rejection properly is that we need to come to terms with our human weaknesses. The reason we fail each other is that we are weak, self-centered at times, and, yes, sinful. While we have the glorious image of God stamped upon our lives, we also have a dark side, a weak side, and a sinful side. The reason that Jesus, God's Son, came into this world was to save us from sin so that we could live and treat others as God intended us to. I'm not offering the fact of our

sinfulness as an excuse for hurting others, but it is an explana-
tion. Instead of taking rejection personally, we need to realize
that people hurt us because of their own faults, not because of
ours. It's also important for us to remember that all of us share
the same weakness of character—we can hurt others too by our
rejection of them.

BASHING BELIEFS

When Jesus first told His followers to shake off the dust, He
was speaking to them specifically about rejection. He told His
disciples that some people would not accept their message and
would ridicule them for their belief in Him as their Savior:
"When you enter a town or village and they do not accept you
or welcome your message, shake the dust off your feet." (See
Matthew 10:14; Luke 10:10–11.)

Bashing beliefs and ridiculing religion is something people are
doing more and more commonly these days. Some comedians
and media personalities are ruthless when it comes to making
fun of people's faith. They preach their misguided notion that
religion is the main cause of war and that religion harms the
world. What a falsehood. History shows that every war has
been started by greed. One nation covets the land and resources
of another and attacks it to make itself richer and more powerful. Faith in God enriches people's lives, and I've found that
most people do believe in God on some level and look to Him
for their sense of purpose, value, and direction in life.

Most humanitarian efforts in our world are motivated by
people's deep faith in God—a faith that causes them to have
compassion for others. Jesus went so far as to say, "Blessed are
you when people insult you, persecute you and falsely say all

kinds of evil against you because of me. Rejoice and be glad, because great is your reward in heaven" (Matt. 5:11–12).

My first job as a young teenager was in a grocery store. One of the other bag boys was a couple years older than me; he also was a bully. When this guy found out I went to a Christian school, he started calling me Moses. He would try to get the other guys to call me Moses to make fun of me. The name-calling really hurt and embarrassed me, but I didn't let it show. I put on a good front and acted as if it didn't bother me even though it did. I decided not to fight back but to try to win the older boy over. The best way to beat a bully is to out-love him. Within a couple of months the boy stopped his attention-getting behavior, and he and I became friends. He was one of those sad people who lift themselves up by putting others down.

I had the privilege one time of traveling to India to speak about my faith. India is a beautiful country whose people are gracious, receptive, and hospitable. During my trip I was invited to speak at an afternoon prayer service at a church in the town of Sivakasi. I was told that extremists often persecute Hindus who become Christians. I was asked to speak on the subject of persecution, something I know nothing about from personal experience, but I addressed the subject as best I could.

I have never felt more inadequate in addressing a group of people in my life. I might as well have been asked to give a lecture on quantum physics. (That's not my strong suit either, in case you're wondering.) After I gave the message, I returned to the church later that day to speak at an evening service. During the singing I noticed a woman on the front row whose face was badly swollen on one side. The woman wore a veil to cover her face, but the swelling was too obvious to miss. I leaned over to the pastor and asked, "What happened to her?"

To my shock he replied, "She attended the prayer service this afternoon. When her husband found out, he beat her."

Abuse is rampant against people of all faiths. Fanatics and extremists practice this worst form of rejection. They bully their way through life, discriminating against anyone who doesn't think and believe like them. They try to beat their world into submission instead of blessing the world through service. Stories such as the one about the tragic suffering of that woman in Sivakasi serve to remind us that we should be accepting of people whose beliefs are different from ours. We should be kind and compassionate to everyone we meet because everyone is going through some kind of pain.

I once read that people are like buzzards, bats, and bumblebees when it comes to the matter of perspective. Here's why. If you put a buzzard in a pen that is six by eight feet and entirely open at the top, the bird, even though it's able to fly, won't leave the pen. A buzzard always begins a flight with a ten- to twelve-foot run, and without space to run, the bird will remain a prisoner in the pen. The bat is a nimble creature in flight, but it cannot take off from a low elevation. If it is placed on the floor or on flat ground, it can only shuffle about helplessly until it reaches an elevated place from which it can thrust itself into the air. Then it takes off with great speed. A bumblebee, if placed in an open tumbler, will stay inside until it dies. Never even seeing the opening at the top, it persists in trying to find some way out of the tumbler through the sides near the bottom. It looks for a way out where none exists until it destroys itself.[3]

Like these creatures that are inhibited by limitations, we struggle with our negative feelings of rejection, never realizing that all we need to do is look up and change our perspective about what has happened to us. You don't have to believe the negative things that people say to you or about you. You don't have to take rejection personally. You don't have to be trapped in the prison of feeling unloved or inadequate. Look up and remember who you are, and free yourself from your emotional prison.

Chapter 14

LIFE IS NOT A SPELLING BEE

Giving Up Perfectionism

W HEN MY SON David Paul was in the fourth grade, he excelled in English. He and one of his classmates were selected to represent their fourth-grade class in a spelling bee for the entire school. On the morning of the competition Barbie and I sat in the school auditorium with all the other proud parents and with the student body. You can imagine how anxious we were to see David do well.

The rules were strict and the competition stiff. The judges gave the students a word to spell. They were to repeat the word out loud and then spell it. However, if even one letter was wrong, the student could not amend the spelling. He or she would be omitted from the competition. For an hour the students spelled and misspelled words until only David Paul and his classmate were left from the original group of about sixty students. The drama built as the two of them spelled one word after another without faltering. After all the assigned words had been used up, the judges took out a big yellow book of words used for school competitions. Both boys continued to spell until the time allotted for the competition expired. The judges called a tie and awarded both boys first place. We were so proud of our son.

During the competition I could not help but notice the sad,

dejected, and embarrassed expressions of some of the children who misspelled a word. These children walked off the platform with slumped shoulders and heads hanging down. One boy in particular started to cry as he walked off the stage in defeat. He had expected to win but hadn't. He had expected to have a perfect performance, but it hadn't turned out that way. In a spelling bee the rule is firm: one mistake, and it's over. There is no second chance. There is no opportunity to correct the spelling when a word is misspelled. It's all or nothing.

The good news is that life is not a spelling bee! We get more than one chance to succeed. The mistakes we make don't exempt us from life. But many people experience life as if it were a spelling bee. They think they have to be perfect in order to be worthwhile, so they live with the constant anxiety that in everything they do, it's all or nothing.

We call this psychological struggle *perfectionism*. Perfectionism is not a healthy pursuit of excellence by which we strive to do our best. The pursuit of excellence is a notable quality and one that is crucial to reaching our goals. In the Bible we read, "Whatever your hand finds to do, do it with all your might" (Eccles. 9:10). The apostle Paul, "Whatever you do, work at it with all your heart, as working for the Lord, not for men" (Col. 3:23). Those scriptures describe a healthy work ethic and a commitment to doing our best for the glory of God and for the achievement of our highest potential.

Perfectionism, conversely, is the process of measuring one's worth on the basis of a flawless performance. In the mind of a perfectionist what we do then defines who we are. The performance is confused with the person. Perfectionists are also called workaholics, or they're known as nice guys who always try to please everyone, or they're labeled martyrs who make limitless sacrifices for everyone else but end up being taken advantage of.

Try This on for Size

You may be wondering if you're a perfectionist. Take a look at these common characteristics and see if they describe you.

The perfectionist believes such faulty ideas as "I have to be perfect to be worthwhile" and "I am only loved when I am lovable." This often starts at home with over-demanding parents who relate to their children with conditional love. Children who grow up in this kind of situation learn to act in certain ways to persuade people to love them.

I played basketball in high school. I had a friend who played at another school who was a great player. After high school he went to play for a Christian college. But when it came to basketball, my friend's father was abusive toward him. I saw his father scream at him from the stands whenever he missed a free throw, even when his team won their games and he scored twenty-two points. If my friend had a bad game, his father would put him on restriction and make him shoot hundreds of shots for practice. My friend was a great player, but he was oppressed by his father. I wonder how much he really loved the game. He once told me that whenever he played a bad game, he feared his father.

Fear of failure is the biggest concern of perfectionists. As far as a perfectionist is concerned, to fail is to be a failure. Perfectionists overreact to their failures and to the mistakes that they and others make. If they make one mistake, they feel as if they will never get things right. They like to go back and fix past performances. They obsess over mistakes, telling themselves, "I should have done this," or, "I must never do that again." Perfectionists can't just let things go when someone they know makes a mistake. They feel the need to give directives about the future: "Next time, remember to do this or that," they tell people after every mistake they make. Of course, none of us can live our lives thinking far enough in advance about the "next time." Life usually catches us off guard, and we can't remember what the perfectionist told us to do next time. Perfectionists only talk about "next time" to help themselves feel as if life will be perfect and to lower their feelings of anxiety about the uncertainty of life.

Perfectionists operate from all-or-nothing thinking. The perfectionist is the straight-A student who falls apart when she makes a B or the athlete who wants to quit because he had a bad game performance. The perfectionist fears mistakes and overreacts to them, wanting to give up altogether. All-or-nothing thinking is also known as the saint-sinner syndrome. Perfectionists either feel like the most spiritual person or the worst sinner of all.

The work habits of perfectionists are compulsive and stressful. Perfectionists overwork and are unable to relax. They put too much time and effort into projects that could be done much faster if they were not perfectionists. Since their work has to be perfect, they waste endless hours on needless details. They do this—unconsciously—to feel important and valuable. Remember, the value of a perfectionist's performance affirms to him his value as a person. Perfectionists tell themselves, "If the job is good and everyone praises it, then I am good and everyone will praise me." But their obsession over details often prevents them from finishing a task. They spend too much time on projects, which in turn keeps them from taking on other projects. So they end up accomplishing less because they waste time on unimportant details. The fact is, perfectionism does not increase one's efficiency at a project but rather lowers it.

Another big issue with perfectionists is control. People who are perfectionists feel the constant need to be in control of themselves—and of everyone else. In short, perfectionists are control freaks. This makes them highly critical of themselves and others. They are constantly frustrated with themselves and others because their standard of perfection is never achieved. You see the trap, don't you? Since perfection cannot be achieved, the perfectionist always falls short and therefore feels frustrated and guilty. Instead of accepting the imperfections of life, they keep pushing, demanding more, and they make themselves and the people close to them increasingly miserable.

Perfectionists think a lot about the future. They are always planning ahead, often in their own minds, because they are always dissatisfied with how things are in the present. If your standard is perfectionism, then you are doomed to a life of coming up short. You will try to go back and undo your mistakes instead of accepting life as it is.

I remember when I recorded my first original music project. My producer told me that a music CD is a photo album of an artist at a particular point in the musician's development. When I listen to that CD now, I want to put it away and never allow anyone to hear it. There are a few good musical highlights on it, but I tend to hear all the flaws. Even with the CD's imperfections, though, I don't want to go back and record it over. It's better for me to accept the CD for what it is and go on to record new projects based on what I have since learned musically.

I do the same thing with the books I have written. Even as I write these words, I am thinking about how my writing style has changed and developed based on what I have learned since I wrote my first book. I don't need to go back and rewrite earlier books simply because I have learned more. But that's what perfectionists do. They want to undo or redo the past. It's better to move on to new ventures than it is to waste time trying to correct the past.

One of the most common characteristics of perfectionists is procrastination. Why do people procrastinate? Because they are afraid of failure. It's not a time management issue at all; it's the problem of perfectionism. Unconsciously we tell ourselves that if we don't start or finish a project, we will never have to face people's final judgment on that project—and again, in the minds of those who are perfectionists, that is the same as people's judgment of them. To perfectionists the performance and the person are the same. If you don't like their work, you don't like them. The best way for a perfectionist to avoid negative feedback is not to finish their work. This explains procrastination.

Perfectionists suffer from depression. This comes from their inability to live up to their own standards, from unrealistic guilt over their imperfections and from a negative self-image. Perfectionists also tend to have three chief concerns: diet, time management, and financial security. They maintain a very clean diet, they are obsessed with being on time, and they worry about their economic stability. They fear criticism, rejection, and disapproval. Perfectionists believe that a perfect performance will insulate them from these painful experiences. Of course, this is untrue, and it explains their inner turmoil and the friction they create in their relationships in demanding so much from themselves and from others.

Perfectionists have some very positive traits. Their pursuit of concrete goals, their attention to detail, and their persistence often make them highly successful. But they can create a lot of collateral damage in the process. This includes their inability to relax, their incapacity to handle failure, and the most glaring fact: perfectionism can never be achieved.

SPIRITUAL PERFECTIONISM

Perfectionism presents a big problem in our relationship with God. Many people relate to God—and they think He relates to them—based on their spiritual performance: how much they pray, give money, or practice good deeds. This is why many people avoid God and religion. They feel like they don't measure up. They think of God as an overbearing, perfectionistic parent or schoolteacher who demands that we do our best and constantly points out our faults.

George Buttrick, former chaplain at Harvard University, would have students come to his office, plop down in a chair, and declare, "I don't believe in God."

Buttrick would respond, "Tell me what kind of God you don't believe in. I probably don't believe in that God either."[1]

The comic strip *Dennis the Menace* paints a good picture of God's kindness. Dennis and his friend Joey were leaving Mrs. Wilson's house with their hands full of freshly baked homemade cookies. Joey looked at Dennis and said, "Gee, Dennis. I wonder what we did to deserve the cookies?"

Dennis replied, "Look, Joey, Mrs. Wilson gives us cookies not because we're nice but because *she's* nice."[2] So it is with God. He loves us because of who *He* is—not because of who we are or what we do. God is love (see 1 John 4:8).

The movie *Playing for Time* portrays the story of Fania Fenelon, a member of an orchestra of Jewish women who were spared the gas chambers at Auschwitz as long as they played well. The lives of these women were reduced to a single proposition:

do well or die.[3] When we make our faith a matter of works, we feel that God is watching every detail of our lives and that, as with these women, our salvation depends on our constant perfection. But God's grace keeps us despite the occasional missed notes or dissonant chords of our lives.

I once met a man who told me that he never sinned—that he had achieved sinless perfection. He told me he had not committed any sins since he had experienced a special work of God in his life. Then he added, "But I have made a few mistakes."

"Yeah," I thought, "and your biggest mistake is thinking that you're perfect." After getting over the initial shock of meeting the world's only perfect person, I replied, "Well, call it what you want." Sins, mistakes, shortcomings, failures—the fact remains that "we all stumble in many ways" (James 3:2).

Our deepest emotional need is to be loved and to love. Only when we are loved are we healthy. When we are loved, we are free to love in return. Perfectionism, however, causes people to think that in order to be loved, they need to perform correctly.

Our need for love is met first and foremost through our parents. If parents are loving and nurturing, children grow up feeling safe and secure. If, however, parents are overbearing, demanding, and unaffectionate, children feel afraid and insecure. When they become adults, children of demanding parents battle anxiety, mistrust others, and basically feel insecure in their relationships. Our relationship with God and our understanding of Him is deeply rooted in the relationship we had with our parents when we were children.

God's love is unconditional. It is not based on our performance. But we grow up learning to perform to gain the love of others. We start when we are small children. Parents are forever trying to make their children perform: "What do you say?"

"Say thank you." "Tell him your name." "Tell them how old you are." Of course children never perform on cue. They intentionally make their parents look bad by refusing to perform. Sadly we go through life performing in order to secure approval, affirmation, and love.

Here are two truths we need to know: we cannot do anything good to get God to love us more. And we cannot do anything bad to get God to love us less. I am not advocating irresponsibility. Our actions certainly have consequences. My point is that the only true constant in life is the love of God. God not only loves us—but also He *is* love!

God's love is eternal. "I have loved you with an everlasting love" (Jer. 31:3) is His word to us. His love has no beginning and no end. God loved us before we were born. His love is not based on our behavior, success, personality, or morality. Listen to this amazing truth: "For he [God] chose us in him before the creation of the world to be holy and blameless in his sight. In love he predestined us to be adopted as his sons" (Eph. 1:4–5). God chose you before the creation of the world. His love was placed on you from the moment that you were conceived, and nothing can separate you from the love of God. When you know that, I mean really know it, you will begin to be free from perfectionism and the relentless pursuit of affirmation, validation, and love.

God loves unconditionally. No strings attached. We have a tough time with that because our love is conditional. We love with strings attached. We try not to, but we do. We look for a return on our investment. We expect love in return, but God doesn't. He loves because He is love. We tend to love "because": "I love you because you're beautiful or because you're rich or because of what you can do for me." We also tend to love "if": "I love you if you're pretty or if you meet my needs or if you change and become the person I want you to be." We tend to manipulate, coerce, and control to get what we want.

God loves "in spite of." He loves us in spite of our sins and our failures. God doesn't love us because He wants or needs anything from us. He loves us because we are His children. "God demonstrates his own love for us in this: While we were still sinners, Christ died for us" (Rom. 5:8). Profound words worth pondering—"while we were still sinners." While we were unlovable, Jesus loved us and gave Himself for us that we might be forgiven. Since we tend not to love ourselves, we conclude that God doesn't love us either. Since we are basically afraid of God and we doubt His love for us, we try to make ourselves lovable to Him the way a child performs for a parent's love and affirmation. Experiencing God's unconditional love is the only cure for perfectionism. "Perfect love drives out fear" (1 John 4:18).

Perfect Families

Families are under tremendous pressure today. We strive to do everything right, only to find ourselves dealing with a host of issues. Home is meant to be a place where love is shut in and strife is shut out. But often the strife and stress are worst at home. Comedian George Burns said, "Happiness is having a large, loving, caring, close-knit family in another city."[4]

A couple asked me if marriages are made in heaven. I replied, "Maybe, but the maintenance of them takes place on earth." Only Adam and Eve had the perfect marriage. Adam didn't have to listen to Eve talk about all the men she could have married, and she didn't have to hear about his mother's cooking.

Marriage is the art of twenty-four-hour forgiveness. Happily married couples overlook each other's shortcomings. You have to learn to accept the imperfections of your husband or wife if you expect your marriage to thrive. Love "always protects, always trusts, always hopes, always perseveres. Love never fails" (1 Cor. 13:7–8). The constant pressure created by one spouse telling the other to change this or change that destroys a marriage. Love means acceptance, not change. Change should come naturally and slowly over time rather than being forced under pressure by one spouse expecting the other to be perfect. Marriages are destroyed by constant criticism, complaints, and demands instead of acceptance, love, and forgiveness.

Gandhi said, "I first learned the concepts of non-violence in my marriage."[5] We need to lower the pressure of perfectionism and raise the power of acceptance. It is so powerful to say to your husband or wife, "I love you just the way you are." When you hear your husband or wife say that, it makes you want to be better and to make changes to improve yourself so you can be the best partner possible.

Kids aren't perfect either, and no matter how well we do at raising them, we cannot ensure that they will not have some problems. Give your kids room to fail. They need to know that you still love them even when they do wrong things. Parents are to guide, encourage, provide for, disciple, train, and pray for their children. But that does not mean that our kids will turn out perfectly. I meet so many parents who are disillusioned when their teenagers have personal problems or get into trouble. "Where did we go wrong?" parents often ask themselves. Quite often the parents didn't go wrong anywhere. Teenagers make their own decisions, and sometimes they make poor ones, even though they have been taught better. Parents need to stop blaming themselves for the decisions and actions of their teenage and adult children. (There's an oxymoron—adult children.)

I worked with a couple whose daughter had gone off the deep end. These parents came to see me in desperation, not knowing what to do. They had raised their daughter in the best private schools and in a good church, and they had cared for her in every way. The girl had been an excellent student and been involved in school athletics. Then she got caught up in drugs and became an addict. Her parents had bailed her out time and time again and put her into one rehab program after the other, but she hadn't gotten better. They were mentally, physically, emotionally, and financially exhausted when they came to see me. Now their daughter was in her early thirties, living in a cheap hotel, and engaged in highly destructive and dangerous behaviors.

Her parents were afraid for her safety and concerned for her welfare, but they felt hopeless. "What should we do? Everything we have tried to do for her has failed!"

I encouraged them to intervene for her one more time. So they went to the hotel and convinced her to come home with them. I met with all three of them a couple days later. This couple's daughter was one of the most delightful people I have ever met in my life. She had a magnetic personality. She talked about her faith and her values, even though they were masked by the residue of the substances in her body. She knew the life she was living did not add up to the values her parents had taught her. I asked her if she wanted help or if she wanted to continue living as she had been. "I want help," she said. "This is not the person I want to be."

I located an out-of-state drug intervention program. This young woman had to commit to the program for a minimum of one year. Her parents paid for her treatment, and she entered that program. During the first few months of her treatment I was in the area where the program was being run. The program didn't allow the residents any visitors for the first six months, but I went to see if I could visit this girl anyway.

I went to the office and inquired about her, and the staff told me that everyone was in session, and besides, even though I was a counselor, I could not see her. So I walked out the door. I was almost to my car when I heard someone call my name. I turned around, and there she was. At the very moment when I was about to leave, her group was taking a break, and she saw me. At times it's so clear that our steps are "ordered by the Lord" (Ps. 37:23, kjv). The young woman and I sat down on the front porch and talked for a few minutes. I encouraged her to become the woman she wanted to be.

She wrote to me from time to time to share about her progress. After a year she got out of that center and went to a halfway house. Then she got a job. I didn't see this girl again for another year, when she and her parents came to see me. She hugged me and then rolled up her sleeve and said, "Look, no needle marks. I'm clean."

You see, her parents had done everything right. They had done everything in their power to be great parents, and that is what they were. But being great parents doesn't ensure that our families will be perfect. Great parents aren't perfect parents, and great kids aren't perfect children. We all dream of having the ideal family, but we have to live with the real family we have and face up to the real world.

We need to stop blaming our parents for being imperfect. We were all experiments for our parents. Parenting is the most humbling experience in life. No one can really prepare a person for it. Parenting is on-the-job training. By the time we finally start to get a handle on how to parent, our kids are grown and leaving the house. We finally have all this knowledge about how to parent, but the nest is empty. Plus, we can't share what we've learned, because nobody wants to hear it!

As a parent I have found it most valuable to quickly admit my mistakes and failures to my children. It is important for us to say, "I'm sorry. I made a mistake. Forgive me." When we apologize for our mistakes, our children will see that people aren't perfect and that families are not based on perfection but on love, forgiveness, and understanding.

God's in Charge, Not You

As I said, perfectionists are control freaks. They try to control things and people because it is a way for them to handle their own anxiety. When they feel in control, they feel less anxious. But when it comes to trusting God, we have to give up control. Control what you can control, and leave the rest to God and to the natural course of life. If we trust God, then we don't have to be in control. God runs the universe, not me. If we believe that He is in control, then why do we need to worry and try to control everything? Why do we feel the need to control the people in our lives if we believe that God is in control?

Jesus made an amazing statement as He suffered on the cross. His last words summed up everything He had come to accomplish: "It is finished" (John 19:30). Being a Christian means resting in Christ's finished work for our salvation, accomplished for us through His death for our sins and through His resurrection. We don't have to add anything to the work of Jesus on the cross. It is finished!

Stop striving for perfection, and start resting in God's perfect plan for your life. We don't work for salvation; we receive it as a free gift. We don't have to do penance for forgiveness; we need to ask for and receive forgiveness as a gift from God. We don't earn eternal life by good works; we receive eternal life as the gift of God. Peace comes from trusting, not trying; from resting, not working.

My own struggle with perfectionism in my relationship with God began to end when I understood this statement found in the Bible: "Therefore, since we have been justified through faith, we have peace with God through our Lord Jesus Christ" (Rom. 5:1). The word *justified* means to be declared innocent, pardoned, forgiven, and righteous in God's sight. We are righteous by faith—by trusting in God—not by works. The result of being justified is that we have peace. Perfectionists are never at peace with God, with themselves, or with others because they can't rest in the grace of God. Their sense of worth is based on what they do and on what they accomplish. They try to make themselves righteous, which is another word for *right* or *perfect*. They want everything to be right in the world.

Righteousness is a gift from God; it's not a work that we do. Listen to this amazing truth: "How much more will those who receive...the gift of righteousness reign in life" (Rom. 5:17). If we receive the gift of righteousness from God, we won't keep striving for perfectionism, and we will reign in life instead of being defeated by feelings of failure, guilt, and low self-esteem.

Rest in God's promise of eternal life and in His promise to provide for you. Relax about the issues that make you anxious. You have no control over them anyway. So many people trust God about their eternal salvation but not for their temporary situations. The God who can take care of our eternity can take care of today. Stop performing for God's love and approval and for the approval of others. Accept God's unconditional love and the gift of being right in His eyes, and you will be able to relax more in life as you rest in Him.

WIN ONE MORE THAN YOU LOSE

A baseball team's season is considered a winning one if the team's wins outnumber its losses—by one game. That's how we need to measure our lives. Significance doesn't come from being perfect but from winning one more game than we lose.

Didn't Jesus say, "Be perfect, therefore, as your heavenly Father is perfect" (Matt. 5:48)? Yes, He did. The first time I read that as a teenager, it disturbed me, because I knew I could never do it. But then I learned what the word *perfect* means. The word that Jesus used does not mean "flawless" but rather "complete" and "mature."[6] With this statement He was also speaking about loving others with the kind of unconditional love that God has for us.

There's another biblical statement on perfection that can be equally disturbing if we don't understand it: "Aim for perfection" (2 Cor. 13:11). This statement means "to restore, to mend, to prepare, and to make one what he ought to be."[7] That we can do! We can't be flawless, but we can finish what we start. We can grow up and mature in love. We can love as God loves. We can mend and restore those things and those relationships that have been broken. We can improve on our deficiencies.

I once heard someone on a radio program say, "We aren't always perfect." I laughed out loud in the car when I heard that. What an absurd remark. We're never perfect. We don't waver back and forth between perfect days and imperfect days. Life is *always* imperfect. People are imperfect. Performances are imperfect.

I heard another speaker use the phrase "the human side of us." What other side is there? That's the only side we have. We don't have an angelic side or a divine side. We are human, plain and simple, and humans are imperfect. The power of God's grace in our lives is not to make us less human and more divine but to make us fully human as He created us to be.

> When I say, "I am a Christian,"
> I'm not shouting, "I've been saved!"
> I'm whispering, "I get lost!
> That's why I chose this way."

> When I say, "I am a Christian,"
> I don't speak with human pride
> I'm confessing that I stumble—
> Needing God to be my guide.

> When I say, "I am a Christian,"
> I'm not trying to be strong
> I'm professing that I'm weak
> And pray for strength to carry on.

> When I say, "I am a Christian,"
> I'm not bragging of success
> I'm admitting that I've failed
> And cannot ever pay the debt.

> When I say, "I am a Christian,"
> I don't think I know it all.
> I submit to my confusion,
> Asking humbly to be taught.

> When I say, "I am a Christian,"
> I'm not claiming to be perfect.
> My flaws are far too visible,
> But God believes I'm worth it.

When I say, "I am a Christian,"
I still feel the sting of pain,
I have my share of heartache,
Which is why I seek God's name.

When I say, "I am a Christian,"
I do not wish to judge.
I have no authority;
I only know I'm loved.[8]

My father was an engineer by trade. Sometimes after our family had eaten dinner together, he would read the Bible to us. He usually read from the books of Proverbs and James. I once asked him why he read so often from those books, and he told me, "Because they're full of common sense, and you kids need some common sense." Well, here's some common sense from James about perfectionism: "We all stumble in many ways. If anyone is never at fault in what he says, he is a perfect man [or woman], able to keep his whole body in check" (James 3:2).

Have you ever known anyone who never said the wrong thing? I haven't. We make more mistakes with our words than with anything else in life. We apologize a lot more often for our words than for our actions. We're not perfect, and we need to face up to our imperfections and to realize that we don't have to be perfect to be worthwhile.

JARS OF CLAY

The apostle Paul said, "We have this treasure in jars of clay to show that this all-surpassing power is from God and not from us" (2 Cor. 4:7). Those two words—*treasure* and *clay*—don't seem to go together. Treasure and gold go together, but not treasure and clay. But these two things create a strange mixture of the treasure of God's power inside a simple, common jar of clay. As believers we all have the treasure of the power of God in us, and yet it is restrained by the clay of our lives. We're going to have to get comfortable with that strange mixture and, yes, even with the contradictions about ourselves. Sometimes we resemble an invaluable treasure, but at other times we look more like a clay jar. We have to get comfortable in our skin and come to terms with the gold and the clay that make up all that we are as a person.

So go ahead and strive for excellence. Set goals and do your best, and remember to accept failure as a part of growing in life. To fail is not to *be* a failure—it is to be human. Don't let your success go to your head or let your failures go to your heart. Get used to failure; it's going to be your constant guide in this life. Minimize it as much as you can and certainly learn from failure—but get used to it.

You're not perfect; only God is. The people you love aren't perfect, so stop expecting them to be. You're not in control of everything, so give up the need to control. Stop trying so much and start trusting more. Stop pressing so hard and start resting more. Learn to appreciate a performance in spite of its flaws. Accept your past for what it is—a portrait album capturing where you were at a certain point in time—and stop trying to undo or redo things. It is what it is.

A story is told of a painter being hired to create a portrait of Oliver Cromwell. The style of the painter, Sir Peter Lely, was to portray his subjects, who were often royalty, in their best light. Cromwell was afflicted with warts on his face, but he had an aversion to any kind of vanity. Lely's desire to enhance Cromwell's appearance did not please Cromwell at all. Cromwell reportedly declared to Lely, "Paint me as I am, warts and all!"[9]

Each of us reflects the image of God in which we are made—warts and all. Accept yourself. Rest in the fact that God loves you and accepts you—just the way you are.

Where do you want your life to go from this point on? What unfinished business is keeping you from moving forward? It's time you decided not to let the past hold you back any longer. Get up! Get over it! Get on with it! Shake off the dust of what happened to you and create a bright, new future. It's not what happens to us that matters the most—it's what we make happen. Remember: the past is resolved when the present is fulfilled.

God promises to help us if we take the next step of faith. Ask Him to help you shake off the dust of hurt, disappointment, and anger. Ask Him to give you faith to believe and hope to expect that life can change. Ask Him to give you the strength to move on with your life. Stop analyzing why something bad happened to you and take a bold step forward. Instead of trying to resolve the past, get on with the business of living today. Focus on what you can change.

God has an incredible future for you. How do I know? He said so Himself: "'I know the plans I have for you,' declares the LORD, 'plans to prosper you and not to harm you, plans to give you hope and a future'" (Jer. 29:11). This is God's promise to you. It's time for you to make this your own plan for your life. Shake off the dust of the problems and pain you have experienced, and begin to take hold of all that God has for you.

NOTES

INTRODUCTION

1. William Wordsworth, "My Heart Leaps Up," http://www.bartleby.com/145/ww194.html (accessed December 20, 2012).
2. Taylor Richardson, "Engineered by God—the Human Skin," ApologeticsPress.org, 2004, http://www.apologeticspress.org/apcontent.aspx?category=9&article=1411 (accessed December 20, 2012).
3. Sean Markey, "20 Things You Didn't Know About...Skin," *Discover*, February 6, 2007, http://discovermagazine.com/2007/feb/20-things-skin (accessed December 20, 2012).

CHAPTER 1—WATCH OUT FOR THAT ICEBERG!

1. Gary R. Collins, *The Magnificient Mind* (Waco, TX: Word Books, 1985).
2. Albert Ellis, "Emotional Disturbance and Its Treatment in a Nutshell," Albert Ellis Institute, http://www.rebt.org/emo_disturbance.pdf (accessed December 20, 2012).
3. "My Life Is But a Weaving," author unknown, as quoted in Corrie ten Boom, *Tramp for the Lord* (Fort Washington, PA: CLC Publications, 2010), 12.
4. Socrates, in Plato's *Apology*, as quoted in Julian Baggini, "Wisdom's Folly," *The Guardian*, May 11, 2005, http://www.guardian.co.uk/theguardian/2005/may/12/features11.g24 (accessed December 20, 2012).

Chapter 2—Don't Get Over It—Get on With It!

1. BrainyQuote.com, "Will Rogers Quotes," http://www
   .brainyquote.com/quotes/quotes/w/willrogers104938.html
   (accessed December 21, 2012).
2. Roy B. Zuck, *The Speaker's Quote Book* (Grand Rapids, MI:
   Kregel Publications, 2009), 25.
3. Oswald Chambers, *My Utmost for His Highest* (Grand Rapids,
   MI: Discovery House Publishers, 1935, 1963, 1992), s.v.
   "August 2."

Chapter 3—Forgetful and Fruitful

1. Lewis Carroll, *Through the Looking Glass: And What Alice
   Found There* (Philadelphia: Henry Altemus Company, 1897),
   157–158, 174. Viewed at Google Books.
2. John Donne, "No Man Is an Island," as viewed at PoemHunter
   .com, http://www.poemhunter.com/poem/no-man-is-an-island
   (accessed December 21, 2012).
3. *Merriam Webster's Collegiate Dictionary*, 11th edition (Spring-
   field, MA: Merriam-Webster, Inc., 2003), s.v. "transcend."
4. Ibid., s.v. "restore."
5. Biblesoft's New Exhaustive Strong's Numbers and Concordance with Expanded Greek-Hebrew Dictionary, copyright ©
   1994, Biblesoft and International Bible Translators, Inc., s.v.
   "'Ephrayim."

Chapter 4—It's Not My Fault!

1. William Glasser, *Reality Therapy* (New York: Harper & Row,
   1975).
2. Socrates, in Plato's *Apology*, as quoted in Julian Baggini, "Wisdom's Folly."

3. Chuck Colson, "It's Not My Fault: A Nation of Victims," Breakpoint.org, August 22, 2002, http://www.breakpoint.org/ commentaries/3045-its-not-my-fault (accessed December 21, 2012).

4. As quoted in *Catholic Post*, "Archbishop Fulton Sheen Dies," December 16, 1979, 14, http://www.allendrake.com/elpaso history/sheen/shncaps1.htm (accessed December 24, 2012).

5. Viktor Frankl, *Man's Search for Meaning* (Boston: Beacon Press, 1992), 75.

6. Max Lucado, *A Gentle Thunder: Hearing God Through the Storm* (Nashville: Thomas Nelson, 1995), xv.

7. Booker T. Washington, *Up From Slavery* (Stilwell, KS: Digireads.com Publishing, 2005), 21.

8. Margaret Mitchell, *Gone With the Wind*, chapter 40, as viewed at WebLitera.com, http://www.weblitera.com/ book/?id=144&lng=1&ch=40&l= (accessed December 24, 2012).

9. Lois Einhorn, *Helen Keller, Public Speaker: Sightless But Seen, Deaf But Heard* (Westport, CT: Greenwood Press, 1998), vii.

10. Gary Tuchman, "Homeless Student on His Way to Cornell," May 24, 1996, http://www.cnn.com/US/9605/24/homeless .scholar/ (accessed December 24, 2012); *Jet*, "Homeless Student, 18, Who Studied on the Subway Gets Scholarship to Cornell University," June 10, 1996. Viewed at Google Books.

Chapter 5—My Life in Ruins

1. "Mercies Never Ceasing" by David Cooper, copyright © 2005 by David Cooper Music (admin. by Discover Life Ministries). Used by permission.

Chapter 6—There's Nothing to Fear but Fear Itself

1. Avalon Project, "First Inaugural Address of Franklin D. Roosevelt, Saturday, March 4, 1933," http://avalon.law.yale.edu/20th_century/froos1.asp (accessed December 26, 2012).
2. ThinkExist.com, "Robert Louis Stevenson Quotes," http://thinkexist.com/quotation/keep_your_fears_to_yourself-but_share_your/14617.html (accessed December 26, 2012).
3. K. Krishna Murty, *50 Timeless Scientists* (New Delhi, India: Pustak Mahal, 2008).
4. ThinkQuest.org, "American President: Benjamin Harrison," http://library.thinkquest.org/08aug/01450/benjaminharrison.html (accessed December 26, 2012).
5. Eileen Lichtenstein, "Top Ten Fears of All Time," *Motivational Whisperers* (blog), August 19, 2011, http://www.motivationalwhisperers.com/members/profile/13/blog-view/757 (accessed December 26, 2012).
6. BibleStudyTools.com, s.v. *"agora,"* http://www.biblestudytools.com/search/?q=agora&s=References&rc=LEX&rc2=LEX+GRK (accessed December 27, 2012).
7. *The Rifleman*, season 5, episode 19, "And the Devil Makes Five," airdate February 11, 1963.
8. BrainyQuote.com, "Winston Churchill Quotes," http://www.brainyquote.com/quotes/quotes/w/winstonchu131188.html (accessed December 27, 2012).
9. As quoted in John Maxwell, *Your Road Map for Success* (Nashville: Thomas Nelson, 2006), 122–123.
10. BlueLetterBible.org, "Lexicon Results: Strong's G5046, *teleios,*" http://www.blueletterbible.org/lang/lexicon/lexicon.cfm?Strongs=G5046&t=KJV (accessed December 27, 2012).
11. TreasuryDirect.gov, "The Debt to the Penny and Who Holds It," http://www.treasurydirect.gov/NP/BPDLogin?application=np (accessed December 27, 2012).

12. Biblesoft's New Exhaustive Strong's Numbers and Concordance with Expanded Greek-Hebrew Dictionary, s.v. *"sophron."*

13. According to Beatlesbible.com: "The Beatles performed five songs on their Ed Sullivan Show live debut. They sang "All My Loving," "Till There Was You," and "She Loves You," in the first half of the programme, followed by an advertisement for Anadin. Ed Sullivan's other guest—Georgia Brown & Oliver Kidds, Frank Gorshin, Tessie O'Shea—followed, after which The Beatles performed "I Saw Her Standing There" and "I Want to Hold Your Hand." (Beatlesbible.com, "The Beatles' First Ed Sullivan Show, 8:00 p.m., Sunday, 9 February 1964)," http://www.beatlesbible.com/1964/02/09/the-beatles-first-ed-sullivan-show/ (accessed December 27, 2012).

14. John Croyle, *Bringing Out the Winner in Your Child* (Nashville: Cumberland House Publishing, 1996), 186–188.

CHAPTER 7—DON'T LET ME DOWN

1. GreatChicagoFire.org, "The Ruined City," http://greatchicago fire.org/ruined-city (accessed December 27, 2012).

2. SpaffordCenter.org, "History," http://www.spaffordcenter.org/history (accessed December 27, 2012).

3. Ibid.; Library of Congress Exhibits, "Family Tragedy," The American Colony in Jerusalem, http://www.loc.gov/exhibits/americancolony/amcolony-family.html (accessed December 27, 2012); MoodyMedia.org, "Songs in the Night—Stories of Beloved Hymns," http://www.moodymedia.org/transcripts/storiesofbelovedhymns.html (accessed December 27, 2012).

4. Library of Congress Exhibits, http://www.loc.gov/exhibits/americancolony/images/ac0006s.jpg (accessed December 27, 2012).

5. Library of Congress Exhibits, "Family Tragedy," The American Colony in Jerusalem.

6. MoodyMedia.org, "Songs in the Night—Stories of Beloved Hymns."
7. As quoted in Jack Canfield, Mark Victor Hansen, Madeline Clapps, and Valerie Howlett, *Chicken Soup for the Soul: Teens Talk Middle School* (Cos Cob, CT: Chicken Soup for the Soul Publishing, Inc., 2008), 238.
8. James L. Noles Jr., "Charles A. Boswell," Encyclopediaof Alabama.org, March 29, 2012, http://www.encyclopediaof alabama.org/face/Article.jsp?id=h-1771 (accessed December 27, 2012).

CHAPTER 8—DON'T LET THE SUN GO DOWN ON ME

1. ThinkExist.com, "Winston Churchill Quotes," http://thinkexist .com/quotation/a_man_is_about_as_big_as_the_things_that_ make_him/182489.html (accessed December 27, 2012).
2. I have compiled this list from various articles I have read over a period of several years.
3. Ibid.
4. ThinkExist.com, "Dr. Laurence J. Peter Quotes," http:// thinkexist.com/quotation/speak_when_you_are_angry-and_ you-ll_make_the_best/214568.html (accessed December 27, 2012).
5. John Rowan Claypool, "The Future and Forgetting," *Preaching Today*, Tape no. 109, as quoted in R. David Reynolds, "The Seven Deadly Sins: Lust," SermonCentral.com, February 2008, http://www.sermoncentral.com/sermons/the-seven-deadly-sins -lust-r-david-reynolds-sermon-on-addiction-118124.asp (accessed December 27, 2012).
6. Billy Graham Center Archives, "Papers of Elisabeth Howard Elliot—Collection 278," http://www2.wheaton.edu/bgc/ archives/GUIDES/278.htm (accessed January 18, 2013).

7. As quoted in Roy B. Zuck, *The Speaker's Quote Book* (Grand Rapids, MI: Kregel Publications, 2009), 144.

CHAPTER 9—UNFINISHED BUSINESS

1. Online Etymology Dictionary, s.v. "resent," http://www.ety monline.com/index.php?term=resent&allowed_in_frame=0 (accessed December 27, 2012).
2. Ralph Waldo Emerson, "Greatness," *Letters and Social Aims* (1876), as quoted in Fred R. Shapiro, ed., *The Yale Book of Quotations* (New Haven, CT: Yale University Press, 2006), 245. Viewed at Google Books.
3. Corrie ten Boom, *Tramp for the Lord* (Fort Washington, PA: CLC Publications, 2011), 57.
4. Jeff Maysh, "'Put a Lid on Your Hatred': Rodney King Says Rioters Who Brought London to a Standstill Won't Solve Anything," *Daily Mail*, August 15, 2011, http://www.dailymail .co.uk/news/article-2026067/Police-brutality-victim-Rodney -King-slams-rioters-brought-London-standstill.html (accessed December 27, 2012); Jim Kavanaugh, "Rodney King Looks Back Without Anger," CNN.com, June 17, 2012, http://www.cnn .com/2012/04/28/us/rodney-king-profile/index.html (accessed December 27, 2012).
5. As related in Howard Bean, "Higher Education," *COMPAN-IONS*, November 2000, http://www.joyintheworld.info/index .html?/teachings/education (accessed December 27, 2012).
6. Robert Frost, "The Road Not Taken," viewed at Bartleby.com, http://www.bartleby.com/119/1.html (accessed December 27, 2012).

Chapter 10—Knocked Down but Never Out

1. QuoteDB.net, "Thomas Edison," http://quotedb.net/thomas
   -edison-%E2%80%93-2000-step-process/ (accessed December
   27, 2012).
2. As quoted in Zuck, *The Speaker's Quote Book*, 183.
3. Lucas Morel, "Lincoln's 'Failures'?," http://showcase.netins.net/
   web/creative/lincoln/education/failures.htm (accessed December
   27, 2012).
4. "Albert Einstein (1879–1955)," Department of Astronomy,
   Case Western Reserve University, http://burro.astr.cwru.edu/
   stu/20th_people_einstein.html (accessed December 27, 2012).
5. Internet Movie Database, "Biography for Fred Astaire," http://
   www.imdb.com/name/nm0000001/bio (accessed December 27,
   2012).
6. John Robinson, "Bob Dylan: The Hibbing High School 'Class of
   1959' Reunion," Telegraph.co.uk, July 23, 2009, http://www
   .telegraph.co.uk/culture/music/bob-dylan/5887887/Bob-Dylan
   -the-Hibbing-High-School-Class-Of-1959-reunion
   .html (accessed December 27, 2012); Collectors-Society
   .com, "The Greatest Songwriter of All Time," message board,
   http://boards.collectors-society.com/ubbthreads.php?ubb=
   showflat&Number=4417051 (accessed December 27, 2012).
7. *Success*, "SUCCESS Legend: W. Clement Stone," http://www
   .success.com/articles/1007-success-legend-w-clement-stone
   (accessed December 27, 2012).
8. Thomas Lake, "Did This Man Really Cut Michael Jordan?",
   Sports Illustrated, January 16, 2012, http://sportsillustrated.cnn
   .com/vault/article/magazine/MAG1193740/index.htm (accessed
   December 27, 2012).
9. H. Jackson Brown, *P.S. I Love You* (Nashville: Rutledge Hill
   Press, 1990), 13.
10. Author unknown.

11. BoxRec.com, "James J. Corbett," http://boxrec.com/media/ index.php/James_J._Corbett (accessed January 2, 2013); Wikipedia.org, s.v. "James J. Corbett," http://en.wikipedia.org/wiki/ James_J._Corbett (accessed January 2, 2013).

12. "I'm Praying for You" by David Cooper. Copyright © 2009 by David Cooper (admin. by Bluebird Publishing Co.). Used by permission.

13. Henry Wadsworth Longfellow, "Elegiac Verse," xiv, in *The Works of Henry Wadsworth Longfellow*, vol. 3 (New York: Houghton, Mifflin, 1910), 278.

14. New World Encyclopedia, s.v. "Michelangelo," http://www.new worldencyclopedia.org/entry/michelangelo (accessed January 2, 2013).

15. *New York Times*, "Edison Sees His Vast Plant Burn," December 10, 1914, http://query.nytimes.com/mem/archive -free/pdf?res=F40614FF3F5C13738DDDA90994DA415B848 DF1D3 (accessed January 2, 2013).

16. Ruth Bell Graham, "Mistakes," *Decision*, February 1, 2006, http://www.billygraham.org/articlepage.asp?articleid=644 (accessed January 2, 2013).

CHAPTER 11—I WANT TO BE POSSIBLE!

1. Author unknown, "I Want to Be Possible," InspirationalStories .com, http://www.inspirationalstories.com/2/264.html (accessed January 2, 2013).

2. North American Society of Adlerian Psychology, "About Adlerian Theory," http://www.alfredadler.org/alfred-adler (accessed January 2, 2013).

3. Norman Vincent Peale, *Power of the Plus Factor* (New York: Ballantine Books, 1978), 58–59.

4. As quoted in "Identity Crisis," in Michael Hodgin, *1001 Humorous Illustrations for Public Speaking* (Grand Rapids, MI: Zondervan, 2010), 847. Viewed at Google Books.
5. Theodore Roosevelt, "Citizenship in a Republic," April 23, 1910, as quoted in Frederick E. Drinker and Jay Henry Mowbray, eds., *Theodore Roosevelt: His Life and Work* (n.p.: National Publishing Company, 1919), 325–326. Viewed at Google Books.
6. *Bits and Pieces*, vol. T, no. 2 (Fairfield: Economics Press, n.d.), 9–11.
7. As related in Brian Bolton, "Desperate Parents," Sermon Central.com, December 2005, http://www.sermoncentral .com/sermons/desperate-parents-brian-bolton-sermon-on -parenting-91152.asp (accessed January 2, 2013).
8. Robert F. Kennedy, "Policy," http://bobby-kennedy.com/rfk policy.htm (accessed January 2, 2013).
9. Jason Zweig, "Meet 'Future You.' Like What You See?," *Wall Street Journal*, March 26, 2011, http://online.wsj.com/article/ SB10001424052748703410604576216663758990104.html (accessed January 2, 2013).
10. Jack Curry, "Teammates Recall Jeter's Journey From Minor Leagues to Great Yankee," *New York Times*, September 12, 2009, http://www.nytimes.com/2009/09/12/sports/ baseball/12jeterteammates.html?_r=0 (accessed January 2, 2013); Benjamin Hill, "'Captain' Jeter Developed in Minors," May 16, 2011, http://www.milb.com/news/article .jsp?ymd=20110504&content_id=18638298&fext= .jsp&vkey=news_milb (accessed January 2, 2013); Jim Randel, "Seeing Your Future," *Active Rain* (blog), October 19, 2009, http://activerain.com/blogsview/1292757/seeing-your-future (accessed January 2, 2013).
11. Values.com, "The Greatest," http://www.values.com/ inspirational-stories-tv-spots/99-The-Greatest (accessed January 2, 2013).

12. GoodReads.com, "Ludwig van Beethoven Quotes," http://www.goodreads.com/author/quotes/40589.Ludwig_van_Beethoven (accessed January 2, 2013).

13. Christine Sipherd Elementary School, "Music Room: Beethoven," http://empire.cyberschool.com/CSE/Department/11-Music-Room/1334-Untitled.html (accessed January 2, 2013).

Chapter 12—To Thine Own Self Be True

1. Human Life Alliance, "A Chronology of Life in the Womb [Fetal Development]," 2005, as viewed at http://www.christian liferesources.com/article/a-chronology-of-life-in-the-womb-fetal -development-1043 (accessed January 2, 2013). Used with permission.

2. Gunter Wyszecki, *Color* (Chicago: World Book Inc., 2006), 824, as quoted in Glenn Elert, ed., *The Physics Factbook*, http://hypertextbook.com/facts/2006/JenniferLeong.shtml (accessed January 2, 2013).

3. "Exploring the Mysteries of the Ear," *Popular Mechanics*, December 1925, 955–958. Viewed at Google Books.

4. NexiumResearch.com, "Digestive System Facts," June 9, 2008, http://www.nexiumresearch.com/2008/06/09/digestive-system -facts/ (accessed January 2, 2013).

5. Discovery Health, "16 Unusual Facts About the Human Body—4: New Stomach," http://health.howstuffworks.com/human-body/parts/16-unusual-facts-about-the-human-body4 .htm (accessed January 2, 2013).

6. Tempe Union High School, "Biology Week 25—Bones and Muscles," http://staff.tuhsd.k12.az.us/gfoster/standard/bbones .htm (accessed January 2, 2013).

7. ThinkQuest.org, "Skeletal System," http://library.thinkquest .org/2935/Natures_Best/Nat_Best_High_Level/Page_Shells/ Skeletals_Shell.html (accessed January 2, 2013).

8. The Franklin Institute, "Blood Vessels," http://www.fi.edu/ learn/heart/vessels/vessels.html (accessed January 2, 2013).

9. Mayo Clinic staff, "Video: Heart and Circulatory System— How They Work," August 5, 2011, http://www.mayoclinic.com /health/circulatory-system/MM00636 (accessed January 2, 2013); Discovery Health, "16 Unusual Facts About the Human Body—10: Blood Distance," http://health.howstuffworks.com/ human-body/parts/16-unusual-facts-about-the-human-body10 .htm (accessed January 2, 2013).

10. Blood Bank of Alaska, "Everybody Has It, Every Body Needs It," http://www.bloodbankofalaska.org/about_blood/index.html (accessed January 2, 2013).

11. Shafiq Qaadri, "Obesity," in *The Testosterone Factor*, http:// www.doctorq.ca/Testosterone-Factor-Obesity-Chapter.html (accessed January 2, 2013).

12. Abhijjit Naik, "Interesting Facts About the Nervous System," Halifax Regional School Board Teacher Webspace, http://hrs bstaff.ednet.ns.ca/holmesdl/Biology%2012/intro%20nervous_ system.htm (accessed January 2, 2013); Robert Sylwester, *How to Explain a Brain* (n.p.: Corwin Press, 2004), 162. Viewed at Google Books.

13. EdHelper.com, "Your Lungs: Simple or Simply Amazing?", http://edhelper.com/ReadingComprehension_54_2487.html (accessed January 2, 2013); WiseGeek.com, "How Do the Lungs Work?", http://www.wisegeek.com/how-do-the-lungs-work.htm (accessed January 2, 2013).

14. Collins, *The Magnificent Mind*.

15. BlueLetterBible.org, "Lexicon Results: Strong's H1564, *golem*," http://www.blueletterbible.org/lang/lexicon/lexicon .cfm?Strongs=H1564&t=KJV (accessed January 2, 2013).

16. PBS.org, "Meet Lucy," http://www.pbs.org/saf/1103/features/meetlucy.htm (accessed January 2, 2013).

17. Jennifer Viegas, "'Ardi,' Oldest Human Ancestor, Unveiled," *Discovery News*, October 1, 2009, http://news.discovery.com/history/ardi-human-ancestor.html (accessed January 2, 2013).

18. Malcolm Ritter, "Doubts Raised on Fossil's Ties to Humans," Boston.com, May 28, 2010, http://www.boston.com/news/science/articles/2010/05/28/scientists_raise_doubts_about_human_link_to_ethiopia_fossil/ (accessed January 2, 2013).

19. Covenant Baptist, Dayton, "The Summation of All Things in Christ," http://www.covenantbaptistdayton.org/studies/Meadows/Ephesians/Eph11_ch2_vs4-10.pdf (accessed January 2, 2013).

20. Robert Burney, *Codependence: The Dance of Wounded Souls* (Cambria, CA: Joy to You and Me Enterprises), 88–89.

Chapter 13—It's Not the End of the World

1. Online Etymology Dictionary, s.v. "rejection," http://www.etymonline.com/index.php?term=reject&allowed_in_frame=0 (accessed January 3, 2013).

2. Book of Famous Quotes, "Famous Quotes About Theater," http://www.famous-quotes.com/topic.php?tid=1212 (accessed January 3, 2013).

3. As related in a sermon illustration by Kelly Benton, "The Buzzard, the Bat, and the Bumble Bee," SermonCentral.com, September 2005, http://www.sermoncentral.com/sermons/the-buzzard-the-bat-and-the-bumble-bee-kelly-benton-sermon-on-faith-general-87982.asp (accessed January 3, 2013).

Chapter 14—Life Is Not a Spelling Bee

1. Philip Yancey, *The Jesus I Never Knew* (Grand Rapids, MI: Zondervan, 1995), 264.

2. As related in Bible Secrets Revealed, "Mrs. Wilson's Cookies," July 17, 2012, http://biblesecrets.wordpress.com/2012/07/17/mrs-wilsons-cookies/ (accessed January 3, 2013).

3. *Playing for Time*, directed by Daniel Mann (Szygzy Productions LTD., 1980), TV movie.

4. BrainyQuote.com, "George Burns," http://www.brainyquote.com/quotes/quotes/g/georgeburn122473.html (accessed January 4, 2013).

5. ThinkExist.com, "Mahatma Gandhi Quotes," http://thinkexist.com/quotation/i_first_learned_the_concepts_of_non-violence_in/148496.html (accessed January 4, 2013).

6. Biblesoft's New Exhaustive Strong's Numbers and Concordance with Expanded Greek-Hebrew Dictionary, s.v. "*teleios*."

7. BlueLetterBible.org, "Lexicon Results: Strong's G2675, *katartizo*," http://www.blueletterbible.org/lang/lexicon/lexicon.cfm?Strongs=G2675&t=KJV (accessed January 4, 2013).

8. Carol Wimmer, "When I Say, 'I Am a Christian,'" copyright © 1988 by Carol Wimmer; http://carolwimmer.com/when-i-say-i-am-a-christian (accessed January 4, 2013). Used by permission.

9. The Phrase Finder, "Warts and All," http://www.phrases.org.uk/meanings/warts-and-all.html (accessed January 4, 2013).

EMPOWERED
TO RADICALLY CHANGE
YOUR WORLD